ANGELS ON EARTH

A GUIDE FOR AWAKENING ANGELS

Parts I & II

Tamara of the Angels
Channeled by Bunny Lang

ANGELS ON EARTH
A GUIDE FOR AWAKENING ANGELS
Parts I & II

Copyright © 2015, Bunny Lang, Angel of Lights Publications. All Rights Reserved.

No part of this book may be reproduced or transmitted in any form, or by any means, electronic or mechanical, now available or developed in the future, without the express written permission of the author who can be reached through Angel of Lights Publications, P.O. Box 153, Pearblossom, CA 93553

ISBN 10: 1719067376
ISBN 13P 9781719067379

Printed in the United States of America.

This is a print-on-demand book. If for any reason you are dissatisfied with the quality, please return to place of purchase for a replacement copy. Contact the Angel of Lights Publications if you have any questions.

Angel of Lights Publications
P.O. Box 153
Pearblossom, CA 93553

*Did you hear the sound? The clang of the bell?
When it rang, the Angels answered,
and Light streamed down from the Heavens.*

A Note and a Blessing

Those who reach for the light of truth to bring truth to others, all prophesy in part. We prophesy in part because we are all individual aspects of our Creator's consciousness and are at varying degrees of this consciousness.

It is of the utmost importance to always be reaching for higher and higher truths. As you climb the dimensions, there will be new experiences. You will be in a wider, brighter, field of consciousness, which carries its own perspective, its own lessons, and its own powers.

One might question, "If Angels can manifest at anytime, anywhere, then why would they need to be born in a human body?" That is a very good question whose answer will reveal much, much more than you could imagine.

Angels are powerful beings. This book is dedicated to the Awakening Angels.

I pray this guide blesses you in many ways.

Tamara of the Angels

TABLE OF CONTENTS
PART I

INTRODUCTION	9.
DEFINITIONS	11.
CHAPTER I	15.
ANGELS ON EARTH	
Powerful Beings of Light	17.
Awakening Angels	21.
Are You an Angel?	23.
Let the Journey Begin	29.
CHAPTER II	33.
STAGES OF AWAKENING	
Introduction	35.
Opening Your Eyes	37.
Swaying	41.
A Personal Experience, and Forgiveness	43.
Flying	49.
CHAPTER III	51.
THE PLAYING FIELD	
The Fallen Consciousness	53.
The Truth of the Angels	65.
The Suns of God	79.
The Collective Consciousness	85.
A Conversation with the Ascended Host and the Forces of Darkness	91.

CHAPTER IV	97.
ANGELIC PRAYERS	
The Entranceway of the Heart	101.
Calling and Claiming One's Angelic I AM Presence	102.
Gratitude	104.
Discernment and Wisdom	105.
Prayer of Self-Acceptance	106.
Healing Anger	107.
Protection	108.
Forgiveness	109.
Mary's Heart for a Peaceful Home	110.
CHAPTER V	111.
EMBRACING THE TREE OF LIFE	
A Story	
CLOSING THOUGHTS	117.
ANGELS ON EARTH PART II	119.

INTRODUCTION

This is not a fanciful book about Angels. It does not ride the surface of understandings that are currently being taught in our world today.

This is a book about the Truth of the Angels. It is a teaching, which explains why we chose to take on human bodies, what our abilities are, and how to awaken those abilities further.

This book covers the playing field of the 3rd Dimension, a.k.a. Planet Earth. There are teachings, which describe the way energy, thought forms, and the collective consciousness create this dimension.

It is critical for us to understand how this dimension came to be the way it is, a low level of Light, so we can change the direction of manifestation upon this planet and increase its level of Light. So many talk about the 5th Dimension. There will be no getting to the 5th Dimension without a large shift in the consciousness of the Beings within the 3rd Dimension.

Because I am from the West, I will reference Biblical verses in, The Fallen Consciousness, in order to explain how these verses are misinterpreted and how their misinterpretation has prevented Co-creators from realizing whom they are, thus keeping them in the seemingly endless cycle of birth and death. One need not be familiar with the Bible to understand these teachings, and I am not setting any religious agenda.

Predominately written for Awakening Angels, this material also contains teachings for those who are further along the path. There are a host of insights, tools and techniques one can use to become aware of one's ego, dissolve its influence, and raise one's consciousness.

The next section includes various definitions of terms and words used throughout this book. If they are unfamiliar to you, becoming familiar with them is advised.

It is my sincere prayer the presented material helps you on your journey whether you are an Angel or not. For, I urge all to familiarize themselves with the complexity of manifestation, and how it rules the 3rd Dimension.

***

DEFINITIONS

Why do we use interchangeable words? Throughout history there have been many teachers, masters, and writers from various cultures, each of them translating their understanding of the universal energies and truths for the time they've lived in. These teachings have been passed around, rewritten, some words used here, and others there. By studying several religions, teachings, and through meditation and reflection, one learns these words are similar in meaning. I will be referencing the realms in the ways I have come to know them.

Those of us who travel the dimensions receive information at the level we can understand and interpret it. The Heavenly Realms do not use the languages of Earth. They send a ray of Light, a thought form, into the 3rd Dimension. We decode it according to our abilities. Things can get confused in the mix at times. What I do know is this: if you want the Truth, you shall have it.

In this material, I will be teaching about the first five dimensions because that is what is needed at this time.

*

Ulmighty: this is how I refer to our, Ultimate Creator.

Dimensions, Planes and Realms: are the same thing. In John, 14:2 Christ said, "In my father's house there are many mansions." These mansions are the dimensions. They are planes of reality separated by levels of consciousness.

1st Dimension: the mineral kingdom. These are the base substances of consciousness. From these materials and other forms can be created.

2nd Dimension: the plant and animal kingdom. Plants, animals, reptiles, etc., have more consciousness than they have been given credit for. This is predominantly due to man projecting his own disconnect from Spirit onto them.

3rd Dimension: the plane of egoic thinking where denser forms of manifestations are seen. This plane houses those Souls who are unaware of their Spiritual Heritage.

4th Dimension: the Astral Plane, also known as, The Emotional Realm. This dimension is the mansion of the Collective Consciousness. It also houses incarnate Beings of a low Light who are either waiting to embody, or who cannot embody because their level of Light cannot reach even the 3rd Plane because of its level of darkness. This is a complex plane, and it is critical to understand its nature. Which will be further discussed in this book.

5th Dimension: the beginning of the Heavenly Realms. The 5th Dimension has many levels of Heaven within it.

Heavenly Realms: beginning with the 5th Dimension and going all the way up to the Heart of our Creator. The Heavenly Realms are all that is of the Light, including all of the Beings who have ascended into higher states of consciousness. There are many levels within these dimensions, for there are many levels of consciousness. The Heavens are referred to as the Heaven(s) because of the many houses, or dimensions within it.

Holy: I suggest you use the word Holy when calling on any being of Light, we cannot assume if we call on help, that it will be given to us from Light Beings, as the forces of darkness are ever standing by to interfere, they simply do not want us here.

Frequencies: Frequencies are vibrations. They are the unseen energies of consciousness.

Light: This word is used quite frequently in this book. In these writings Light is capitalized because it is referring to high states of consciousness in the Heavenly Realms. It is a matter of honor and respect. There are certain terms and words that simply do not follow

Earthly ways of representation. If I say, Call in the Light, I am saying, call in the highest form of consciousness you are capable of. When I say, Stand in the Light, or Stand in the Truth of the Light, I am saying, stand in the Truth of the highest form of consciousness you can attain, and be firm in your conviction of it. Do not be swayed by levels of egoic thinking.

Truth: capped because it is the reality of the Heavenly Realms. It is consciousness devoid of egoic thinking.

Energetic Bodies, Levels, Fields, Realms: The basic energetic bodies are the Physical, Emotional and Mental Realms. These bodies can be seen as levels as they lay on top of each other, and they can been seen as fields because they are vast. They are also referred to as Realms because of their individual natures.

Thought Forms: pre-manifested beliefs that are gaining etheric weight in either one's personal consciousness, or the Collective Consciousness. These forms will eventually manifest depending upon the intensity put into the thought form.

Spirit: individual or collective Divine connection, either to one's I AM Presence, or the overall identification with the Heavenly Realms.

I AM Presence: the Truth of who we are, our Spirit, our Light, our Consciousness without form.

Co-creator: A being who, either unconsciously, or consciously, creates their life according to their level of awareness. Co-creator also means creating in union with others.

Egoic: Ego thinking is man's common daily life thinking. Thinking that is based upon believing the three dimensionality of existence is the supreme reality, life on Earth, as we commonly know it. Egoic thinking stems from a belief that one *is* their body, and thus fights for survival of that body. It defends and justifies its separation from our Creator, and others, because it carries the beliefs of, guilt and punishment, which it then projects onto the world. Egoic thinking is highly susceptible to the Collective Consciousness, and adds to it readily.

***

CHAPTER I

ANGELS ON EARTH

*There comes a point when we must decide
if we're going to go all the way
and become who we are.*

POWERFUL BEINGS OF LIGHT

There are an immense number of books and chronicles written about the Angels, but in many ways, we have been homogenized in society. We have been known to be comforters, healers and helpers with a type of gentility assigned to us, which overrides our true significance.

Some of the artwork depicting the Angels shows us in animated, somewhat passive states. At times, we are even portrayed with a lustful type of sexuality. We realize the Souls on Earth do not truly understand who we are, so we do not blame them, or spend much time obsessing about this issue. What is on our mind is getting the Co-creators of this planet aware of whom they are. To do this, we must know the Truth of who we are.

Angels are powerful Beings of Light and we came here to Call the Light, to Anchor the Light, and to Direct the Light. We also serve in other ways, the traditional, and the not so traditional. We are privy to various techniques simply because we were created to use them. After all, we are servants of the Most High.

Co-creators can raise their consciousness and anchor Light. However, Angels were created for this purpose with a consciousness that already holds a high degree of Light. We could not move through the dimensions and carry out our assignments if we did not have a high level of consciousness. Each dimension carries within itself it's own state of consciousness. We are adept at many of these states because we were created to move through them. Depending upon our own stage of development, some dimensions will be more familiar to us than others.

When we are on a long-term mission, like taking on a body on Earth, we learn the dimension in detail so we can teach the Souls who live there. It is easier for us to grasp what is going on and to bring information down from the Heavens. We are always growing in the Light. I can say we are always growing in confidence because Angels naturally Love to be close to the Light. Being away from the Light is foreign to us, and uncomfortable. The whole notion of fallen Angels will be explored through this material and it may change the way you think of Angels.

Angels live simultaneously inside and outside of a dimension. When outside of a dimension, let's say the 3rd, Planet Earth, we can see past the illusions many Co-creators believe. When we are inside, our frequencies become highly tuned to our environment, which makes us extremely empathic. Due to this level of empathy, we are full of Loving compassion and have a desire to help Co-creators overcome their sorrows and break through the many illusions that are keeping them from knowing who they truly are. Angels can also get stuck in the mire if we allow our emotions to rule us.

We work with the Ascended Host in the Heavenly Realms. Angels on Earth communicate to each other whether they are aware of it or not. The more our consciousness is raised and we claim who we are, the easier it will be for us to connect and use our powers in unison.

Archangels are High Masters in the Angelic Kingdoms. Their Light is developed to such a degree that they can be called to many places at once. They generally do not take on a human body. Because of the Power of their Light, they are much more effective working through the unseen worlds.

Music, color, and movement are manifestations of vibrating Light, which Angels are masters of. Angelic artists are able to provoke deep inner feelings of resonance with the Divine. Holy Angel's hearts are open to beauty and they simply cannot create images or sounds that are negative in nature. If called upon, an Angel can send those vibrations to a Co-creator who will then manifest the energy through their own distinct personality. Much like being inspired by a muse.

There are times when Angels volunteer to move into darker energies within the fields of art, entertainment, business and politics. Remember, we wear many masks; play many roles. This can be tough on an Angel, particularly an Awakening Angel. When Awakening Angels are immersed in darker forms of consciousness, we can become torn between what we know to be Light and the darkness of the arena we are in. We may lose touch with our purpose. Once we realize we were sent into this arena because we are needed, we get off our own backs and surrender to our mission. Sometimes it is only our presence, which is needed. We do not have to say or do anything, Light speaks for itself, and Light spreads. In time, our field of service will shift. This generally happens when we've completed our mission.

It is important to not judge one's area of service. This happens in the beginning because we were taught that Angels are specific types of Beings. These teachings are limited and do not cover the scope of our service.

The rest of this chapter is dedicated to those who may be wondering if they are an Angel. I send those who are Awakening, a Special Blessing of Light. May your sensitivity to your Angelic Self be heightened and your many questions answered.

***

AWAKENING ANGELS

If you are an Awakening Angel, you probably have a lot of questions. One being, "Is this for real?" Two being, "What am I doing on Earth?" and not necessarily in that order.

The entire planet has been shifting to be able to hold higher frequencies of Light, which began to quicken with the Harmonic Convergence, the time when co-creators and Angels became more awake due to the work of those whom came before us. From that time, more Light has been coming onto the planet from the Seven Rays and the Ascended Host. This Light causes our bodies to vibrate at higher speeds and in turn raise our consciousness. We begin to question what we have known to be true about reality and begin to reach out for help in the further raising of our consciousness.

Angels have specific roles when it comes to lifting the consciousness of the Souls who live here; aiding in the release of the dense, negative energies that the planet has absorbed. Your becoming aware of who you are better enables you to use your gifts to help shift consciousness on a larger scale, and aid those who are having difficulty making the transition into Light.

If you are awakening, you will be having many experiences that others may not know how to help you with. I suggest you make a practice for yourself and continue to connect to your, I AM Presence, your Holy Angelic Self, and ask God for guidance. By now you most likely have a favorite Ascended Master whom you speak with, it may even be a fellow Angel. The Heavenly Realms are always gracious to send us a teacher. We are meant to know who we are, and so there is much assistance given to us. It is up to us to take this assistance seriously and awaken so we may be of service, which is why we are here.

Throughout your life, you will be lead to the specific techniques you are to study. These are the tools you will be using to shift Light, give messages, heal, and more. It is important to be flexible and leave a study when it is time. Angels do not often stick with one teaching. We tend to move around because we learn rather quickly and cover a lot of areas in our service. You will know when it is time. Please do not feel you need to rush this process, trust that you are being taken through training, and continually give yourself up to thee highest truth you can muster to live, much soul searching is needed.

Awakening isn't something you, the you, you are familiar with, is doing. Your Earthly egoic mind is not saying it wants to wake up to be an Angel. It is happening because the you that is an Angel is saying that it's time.

This can be very confusing. What we know about Awakening Angels is currently limited. If we were to run out and tell our friends and neighbors we believe we are an Awakening Angel, it may ruin any Earthly credibility we may have. We probably already seem a little, out there. The Souls on this planet are only beginning to awaken themselves. Their interpretations of life, and particularly Angels, are far away from what the actual facts are.

What *is* important is for us to awaken and *claim ourselves*. The moment we claim ourselves we will feel the power of who we are. The fact that we are Angels will be undeniable, and we will fall in Love with ourselves, and our mission.

ARE YOU AN ANGEL?

When the idea first came to me, I was both very curious and very cautious. The idea of being an Angel is very magical. They fly, they heal, they appear then disappear. It surely is an exciting prospect to think you're an Angel. At the same time, it felt a little bit like another fad in the world of men. So, I approached the idea with reserve. Being cautious means not believing everything one hears, but discerning for oneself. I urge you to be cautious in your seeking of Truth.

Do not judge Angels by anything in this world. There is no hard and fast rule regarding what an Angel looks like, such as hair color or the shape of a face. This is funny to an Angel because Angels are masters of disguise, and for very good reasons. Angels bring the Light in whatever way they are called to. There are Archangel's such as, Archangel Michael, Uriel, Raphael, Gabriel, and Ethereal who have been known to specialize, but that does not make them limited by any means.

In one moment an Angel can send healing energy to a hurting Soul, and the next they can send a beam of Light aimed to destroy a negative thought form half way across the planet.

No seminar or book, although they can guide you, can tell you if you are an Angel. I can give you a more in depth understanding of Angels, which can help you on your path of discerning the Truth for yourself. However, the only way you are going to know for sure is by asking your higher self, your I AM Presence and trusting what you receive. The most direct way is to ask for an experience, and you will probably ask for more than one. This will help ground you in the truth of who you are. A sample prayer could be, "I call upon my I AM Presence, my Holy Christ Self, to give me discernment and a direct experience of my True Self. Am I an Angel?"

If you are anything like me, asking this question may feel pretty bizarre. The idea of Angels on Earth is so foreign to us. Though we may entertain the idea, we mostly entertain it in the way that Angels appear and disappear. We don't generally think of them living among us. Ask you must. If you are an Awakening Angel, it is critical for you to know who you are. As awkward or embarrassing as it may feel, one simply needs to know so one can claim themselves and move on.

If the answer you receive is a yes, this may bring up many reactions. One may feel exhilaration, doubt, or confusion, for it is a large shift in consciousness. I suggest you keep on asking and contemplating. Trust you will receive the answers to your questions. You are meant to know. When you do know, *Claim It*, and keep claiming it. Ask for your name; you have an Angelic name. Trust this name and use it as you call in your Angelic I AM Presence.

*

There is also a bit of fact-finding you can do, as this is what has helped me teeter toward the belief for myself.

When I look back through my life, there have been some very profound messages that have come across my path indicating who I am. These messages were not sought after, for I never even thought about being an Angel. These messages would just pop out of nowhere, and left me very curious as to their meaning. Because they were out of the ordinary, I simply filed them away in my, Hm, That's Odd. I Wonder What It Means, memory bank and went on with my life.

I have elected not to share my direct experiences. In the beginning of my own awakening I had read what someone else's were and it caused a mass of confusion in my consciousness. I questioned the Heavens as to why I didn't have these types of experiences. Because I didn't have a particular type, I believed I could not be an Angel. Comparisons, comparisons. They can be dangerous and take us off the path.

*

If you are an Angel, you mostly likely grew up questioning everything you see. Adults of many types, authority figures, rules. We question our family, and family structures in general. We are curious as to how people relate to each other. We question institutions, religions, politics, and entertainment. We study our culture, our country, our world, in order to learn it from the inside. We question it endlessly, weighing it against the internal Light we know, the Truth we live by.

We mind when there is disorder. What is disorder in the Heavenly Realms? Anything less than the full Light of love. Less than that, one cannot cross the border and enter the 5th Dimension, Heaven.

Angels are Light Bearers. We uphold the Light. We manifest this Light in order and Harmony, which is why we can glide through the dimensions. The vibrations of sound and color.

We are sensitive to the suffering of others. When an Awakening Angel feels the suffering of others, they may get angry at any injustice that caused it. Awakening Angels don't understand the thinking that creates injustice. These feelings of anger are there because we know there is Love and there is Life. This is what causes us to question our own actions, to check our own thinking; to be Clear in the Light. We want to Live in the Light. We realize we do not need to fear, because we are not alone. We are in communion with all of Heaven.

We learn that in this order, in this life, one does not fight flesh and blood, but fights against the powers and principalities in the air, in the Collective Consciousness.

When we see that the world is blinded by the dark cloud that inhabits the Collective Consciousness, we understand. Co-creators do not know what they are doing. If they did, we believe, they would make another choice. We are from the Light. Therefore, we can see.

More questions. Questions that lead us up the road, the road we already know, because we are meant to know. What is this road we know? It is our connection to our Creator. The Spirit Light living within us.

Angels are sensitive to energy. We are drawn to energetic movement whether in sound, color, or healing.

Are we perfect? No. We didn't come here to be perfect. It's rather difficult to continually stay awake in the 3rd Dimension. It's all the pollution. Thought-forms and manifestations. Actually, perfection is an unrealistic expectation because consciousness is always expanding. Unconsciousness has a darker vibration. It is uncomfortable.

An Angel can get caught in the drama. Sometimes, this is exactly what is needed. This is how we learn the playing field. The way man moves. The way Spirit moves. What is the Truth? Seeking for the Truth, we will naturally be drawn to Love in all of our endeavors. Even if we stumble, we continue to reach for the Light. When we reach for the Light, we come back to ourselves, and we teach others how to come back to themselves.

*

Currently, the presence of Angels living on the Earth is being talked about more and more. Some calling them, angelic-humans.
I must state, I am not crazy about the phrase. I feel it confuses those who are actual Angels awakening on Earth. Angelic-human implies one is a human with angelic tendencies, or characteristics. As you read further into this guide you will realize just how sophisticated Angels actually are. We don't have angelic tendencies, we *are* Angels.

Will you be able to identify an Angel living in a human body?

It will take some work to be able to see the Truth of any form. In order to see clearly one must, first and foremost, step out of a conditioned mindset, develop intuition and discernment, and be open to the experience. Taking these steps will help you in many more areas than in the seeing of Angels.

As it stands, many probably already sense the Light of an Angel on

Earth, realizing there is something in those deep, penetrating eyes, but they just can't put their finger on it. That saying, "You may be entertaining Angels unawares" goes deeper than you know.

***

LET THE JOURNEY BEGIN

Some of the questions I ask in the following material may seem applicable to many Beings of Light. However, there is a difference between a Light Worker and an Angel.

A Light Worker is a Co-creator who is beginning to understand both, who they are, and how manifestation works. They live in this dimension to grow and serve. Angels were created to serve the Ascended Host and the Co-creators in any dimension we are called to. One can say Angels are created with a high degree of consciousness while Co-creators are created to grow in consciousness. This is the main reason we feel periodic frustrations with Co-creators. We wonder, "Why don't they just get it?"

Angels do not move at the beck and call of Co-creators whims. Angels realize when Co-creators have these whims, they are off the path; an Angel has no obligation, nor desire, to serve selfish ends.

You will know if you are an Angel by your confusion in the way the world runs, and you may experience depression or anger toward it's destruction and negativity.

I suggest you sit in a quiet place and jot down the various experiences you have had, the messages that have come across your path, the intuitive leadings; the voice of your own Spirit. Write down your gifts. What are you known for time and again? Journaling, and journaling your prayers, will help you in many ways.

Here are some questions you may want to ask yourself.

Are you able to consciously access higher states of consciousness and bring that information down to Earth? This is different than channeling. Channels must step away from any identification with self in order to allow the information to come through. Angels can do this without stepping away from themselves. This is not being psychic. Our information comes from the Heavenly Realms and not the 3rd and 4th Dimensions.

Have you felt great passion and a desire to speak out about injustices toward humanity, and against false teachings?

Have you felt compelled to write down a teaching, warning, or even tell someone something they may not want to hear, or what you may not want to tell them? If you are an Awakening Angel, this can be particularly hard to learn in terms of balancing one's anger in expressing Truth. Currently on this planet, there are not many examples of speaking the Truth in Love. However, in having the desire to Love, one learns how to come from the Truth, how to speak the Truth. It is not always placing flowers at one's doorstep, and this is hard to discern for an Awakening Angel. Be patient with yourself. The Ascended Host will guide you.

Do you feel that new discoveries either in science or metaphysics cause you to roll your eyes because this information is very obvious to you? You just know it and you really are not concerned with how you know it because it resonates with every fiber of your being? You might even get a little miffed because of the obviousness of it, and the fact that another being is creating seminars and books on a subject that to you is second nature. Try not to get too upset. You will not be left out of the Circle of Appreciation for who you are, and you have come to bring your own gift into the world. In the end, the more others know, the more they can grow in the Light, and this benefits the One and the Many.

Do you have a Heart of compassion that longs to see the healing of others whether in an emotional or physical aspect? Do you go out of your way to comfort and give of yourself to those who are wounded? Do you just instinctively know what to do?

Are you interested in working in the realms of the unseen rather than the seen, such as, energy healing, distance healing, or telepathic communication? Do you feel you can easily connect to others through long distances without the use of phones, internet, or other technological devices?

Are you an artist who creates beauty through poetry, art, or music? Do you use colors and tones which are uplifting and inspirational?

Are you close to nature; can you speak with animals and other forms of consciousness within nature?

Do you have energetic sensations that you do not know how to explain, or even work with? Maybe just the opposite, you have the ability to understand energy, sensing and using energy comes naturally to you. Are you empathic?

Are you able to understand high levels of spiritual teachings, and absorb them quickly?

Are you sensitive to noise pollution, i.e., shopping malls, crowds, flashing lights, harsh music, television, cell phone and computer radiation?

Do you feel a strong sense that the Earth is not your true home? I know this question gets asked a lot, and by now it's probably a mute point considering you are reading this material, for you would not be drawn to it if you felt comfortable in the 3rd Dimension.

Do you have a desire to protect others from harm?

Do you feel a strong need to protect that which is Just and True? An Awakening Angel can get confused about what this means, 'Just and True'. 3rd Dimensional definitions on this are actually limited. Yet, there is still a sense, a very strong sense, that the Truth must be protected, that innocence must be protected. An Angel knows the Truth is always in the Light, in our connection to our Creator.

*

I hope this information has helped you understand the various ways Angels operate. In same, I hope these questions have helped you in some way discern the Truth for yourself.

Ask without expectation or attachment. Be open, and the answer will be revealed to you.

Remember, it's really not about being an Angel or not being an Angel, although the idea is very fun, indeed. It truly is about growing in the Light and being in service to the One and the Many in extending that Light. We always find our happiness in who we truly are. Be in joy, you are created! You are alive! Celebrate Life rather than the form.

Whatever form your Light takes, I urge you to continue reading as the following information will help you both understand and navigate the energies on Planet Earth.

If you are an Angel on Earth, welcome to the Truth of who you are.

***

CHAPTER II

STAGES OF AWAKENING

*Though I may fall in error,
in humility I climb.
In Light, I reign.*

INTRODUCTION

When we descend into lower levels of vibration, into the denser forms of matter, it is more challenging to remain connected to who we are. Not only because of the level of density, but also because of the quick thrust into, and magnetic pull of, this dimension. A bit disorienting in and of itself, and then, the journey to learn this new world begins.

The amount of fog/darkness in the Collective Consciousness in this world creates many beliefs that must be broken through, and this can take some doing, depending upon how much Light is on the planet at the time of our birth.

Being born into this dimension, experiencing the same suffering that others go through, gives us a clearer understanding of our service.

Being on Earth gives Angels the authority to hold the Light in this dimension for the span in which we've chosen to serve. This gives us the unique strategic positioning to Call down the Light in various places and at various times, and to Command that Light in a way that will dissolve, or even shatter negative thought forms in the Collective Consciousness.

There always has been, and there always will be Angels on Earth.

***

OPENING YOUR EYES

The song, "Dr. My Eyes," by Jackson Browne, reached into my Soul at an early age. Through it, I felt the pain of my life, the unspeakable sorrow I had to endure in order to learn the ways of men. Music is one of the most significant ways I can reach in and touch, not only my own Soul, but also the Heavens.

Most likely, you have been opening your eyes for quite some time now. Questioning reality in a world that takes it at face value can be a lonely proposition. The play, although simple in it's understanding once you realize the truth of it, is a complex mind field while you are entrenched in it. Learning and mastering the way the mirror portrays its manifestations is part of our job. It enables us to be able to navigate through the playing field, to help others rise to that, simple understanding.

Opening one's eyes is only the beginning. It can be risky. In order to gain a new understanding or perception, one must let go of what they once believed. This new perception leads to another, and yet another. One might find them selves alone, a bit like Alice in Wonderland wondering where they are or what will happen next.

During this time, it is critical that we establish a connection to our Angelic I AM Presence. This connection will be the strength in which we can handle the shift in perceptions that occur. We will question virtues; what is right, what is wrong, or what is Holy.

As our perceptions shift, there may be fewer and fewer persons in our current circle that see what we see. Our common conversations with friends will change. We may become more sensitive to the sound of their voice, and through this understand their intentions, feel their sorrow, or know them in a much deeper way. Perhaps even more than they know themselves.

We may notice others views may be based on outdated ideas coming from one's upbringing and/or the Collective Consciousness. We may experience disappointment, or a sense of loss when we realize others do not want to give up the sense of security they receive from false beliefs. They may cling to them, or defend them. Many are afraid to buck the system for fear of losing a relationship, a job, or what they may consider to be their identity.

At times, common interests among those living on Earth can be devoid of Light. Some are fixated on exterior pleasures; society supports these, and even encourages them.

The relationship we have with our Angelic I AM Presence is paramount to any other relationship we can have. This is our strength, our life boat. There are times when we simply cannot lean on a friend, family member, or another's point of view for the answers we seek, or on an action that needs to be taken. This can cause all manner of judgment against us if we do not believe or behave in a manner that is expected of us. We may even question ourselves because the reality we are coming to know is vastly different than the one we are leaving. Over time, it becomes a familiar practice; asking ourselves if it is best for us to comply with the status quo, or take the leap into individuation.

At the same time, becoming detached to another's life lessons can be confusing to an Angel who has heightened empathy. It can feel like we're abandoning those around us. Yet, we learn that there is a time to use our empathy and a time when we are to pull back. This pulling back may come from our intuition, or it may come from the Ascended Host. Remember, we are not in control of everything. We serve, and service does not always mean to Heaven what it means on Earth.

If we do not have a solid, grounded, daily practice to connect and reconnect with our Holy Angelic Selves, we can get sucked into the quagmire and even get lost. Once we are in deep, it can take us some time to reconnect and move through the sense of guilt that may come from our falling away. In the time we are swimming in the mud of the lower vibrations, we may make mistakes, get confused, hurt another, get into addictions with food, cigarettes, television. We may numb ourselves because we can't find our way out. We may wonder what happened, how did we get here, and are we really an Angel after all? This is a very sad time. It causes all manner of doubt.

It is important for us to remember that we are living in a lower level of vibration, and it will be a common occurrence for us to get sucked in while we are awakening. It is vital for us to remember that we are learning, and while we are learning we are teaching others, even if it doesn't seem like it. To have expectations that we are to be perfect from the get-go is unrealistic. Heaven isn't judging us. Heaven is calling us. We respond by continuing to reach for the Light regardless of how far we have fallen.

In order for us to hold Light, we must continue to draw it into ourselves and extend it outward. Extending it is not necessarily the endless giving of one's energy in a sort of idealistic fantasy of what Love is. Extending it outward is often saying no to false beliefs, or fear. Creating a boundary, an aura of highly refined Light where darkness dare not penetrate. Standing firm in this provides an example for others who may want to be free, but feel they do not have the strength.

It is also important for us to be gentle with ourselves, to forgive ourselves for not living up to our own perceived perfection, to mourn our losses, and to embrace our path.

It will not be all pain. When we begin to move out of the mud and start to see the Light, we will be in joy. We feel free knowing the illusion we have overcome is another string on our bow. We are elated in the revelations we have received. Our fascination with Life will be renewed and we will begin to understand in deeper and deeper ways, the Truth that the reality we are moving away from is but a shadow.

As we realize the connection we have with the Heavenly Realms and the Souls of those on Earth, we learn we can heal much through the Entranceway of the Heart. This becomes real to us. This is when we begin to really strengthen our ability to move through the dimensions. We begin to believe in our gifts and realize that sometimes we are much more useful moving through the unseen world than we are moving through the world that is seen.

Trusting ourselves, this is where we are headed. Knowing our selves, this is our path. Keeping connected to our Angelic I Am Presence is the key to all doors and the mantle of our strength.

(The chapter, Angelic Prayers, will help you center yourself in your Angelic I AM Presence.)

***

SWAYING

As part of your mission, you most likely have had many experiences in order to understand the way this dimension operates. You may have struggled through a rough and tough home life, had a serious illness; perhaps were even caught up in fame and fortune. There may have been times where you felt like giving up, and giving in.

As an Awakening Angel, you probably have been learning many skills in various areas. This is due to your need to be flexible within the playing field. For Spirit will move you this way and that in order to fill many areas with Light. You may be called to work as a chef, and then all of a sudden you are flying to Spain. Your friends and family might think you are crazy. The only way you know you are not crazy is because you have gained a conscious awareness of how Spirit, your Angelic I AM Presence, or the Ascended Host, speaks to you personally. These will be consciously directed choices, not stress induced mania.

Once we know how spirit speaks to us personally, we will be able to discern between impulsive actions and intuition. Impulse can be driven by fear, denial, or the need to escape. Intuition guides with various growing intensities, a sense, a vibe, a gut feeling. At times we can be lead to act quickly, and when this happens, we know it is true spiritual guidance because we have learned to feel into it over time, and have become accustomed to its messages. The sooner we learn that our higher self, connected to spirit is trustworthy, the easier it will be, if, we are willing to listen. Now I say, "Ok, I release what I want in this, please guide me to do what is best for this situation."

We all hear our own thoughts. High Spirits of the Light can send us messages or information. So can the thought forms in the 4th Dimension. They love to get inside your head. Your job is to tell them, No, and escort them to the Light. With skill, you will become aware of them immediately; simply shine your Light upon them, and viola! In the wink of an eye, they are gone. This is the goal, to work with Life as energy.

You may have experienced the darkness that comes through people who are greatly affected by the cloud, the veil. They are trying to control Life because they are consumed with the fear of life, survival, expectations, even death. You had to live among them while breaking out of your own shell. Whatever it is that you have experienced, at one time or another it has pulled you out of that realm called, Peace on Earth. As in, where is it?

This question is the question you are being asked to ask, yourself. Where is Peace on Earth?

If you are looking for something it must be missing. Your job is to find out what is missing in the arena you have been sent into. Your job is to find it and discern it's psychological and spiritual layers, then work within those patterns finding the best way to add Light, so as not to add too little, or too much. Too little will not be effective. Too much will cause a massive shift; Beings who are affected by this shift may not be able to handle it. This could shock them and cause them to retract even further. We must always honor another's Free Will. We simply cannot go around trying to lift others up to dimensions they either do not want to go to, or who are afraid of going to, regardless of the fact that we know it is a happier place.

During this time, awakening Beings of Light will vacillate between the old world and the new world, so to speak. Practical life on the 3rd Dimension may take over while breakups happen, or a job changes occur. One is beginning to see that they are being moved about, and put in position, learning and shifting Light as we go.

Our job is to go where we are sent, and to add Light to these dark places. When one lives in the darkness, they do not see the Light. They do not often see their choice between Spirit and egoic thinking. It is our job to show them there is a choice, by being the Light. This will give them the opportunity to make their choice a conscious choice.

As Neo says in the Matrix, "I'm gonna show these people what you don't want them to see. A world without rules and controls..." I do not reference this as an outward cry to the government in some type of revolutionary act. However, it is a revolutionary act in the realm of Spirit. And this occurs when one lives and breaths in the Light. Become a Living example. Walking the walk because you know the walk. You are the walk. You have not only earned what you know, but you are feeling so free from the confines of life in the 3rd Dimension, you would have it no other way. You have earned the, Power of the Light, and you Wield that Light.

*

Try to be patient with yourself. Try to understand you are swaying because you are learning. You are waking up. No one in the Heavenly Realms is going to shake you in your bed, trying to quickly wake you as if there is a fire and it's life or death. Although this may happen from time to time in instances where some one needs to, 'snap out of it'. But these are few and far between. The Heavens flow. And we can flow with them when we trust that we are, in fact, wanting to be in the Light. And as long as we want to be in the Light, our prayers will be answered.

*

"In Truth you are always the Light, even when you slip and don't remember.

  Just pull yourself back up into the Light". -- Jesus
It is the intension of our Hearts that brings healing. It is the intension of our Hearts that brings Love to Earth.

***

A PERSONAL EXPERIENCE, AND FORGIVENESS

I went to bed last night carrying much sorrow. These past couple of months have been heart wrenching. I know I will never be the same from it. I've been confused, hurt, grieving, angry, and the cycle just continued. During this experience, those whom I confided in rushed me toward forgiveness. I felt as if I were just catching my breath from the blow I had been delivered, and their expectation caused me much anguish.

Going through the daily routines of life were overwhelming to me. I could not work on this book, which added more shame. How could I be drawn into these heavy emotions and write a book about being an Angel? It just seemed absurd to me. Laying in the dark, I felt as if I had finally collapsed. I called out to Jesus who helped me so much when I was young. I had to surrender what I was afraid of surrendering. I had to step into the unknown and trust my intentions, trust my Heart, and give the rest of it to Jesus and the Ascended Host.

I woke up this morning and had no choice but to deal with some important paperwork. There was a pile of letters and bills sitting on my desk. One by one I began to sort them. What slipped out of the confusion was a letter. It was strange. There was no logo quickly identifying who sent it. The date and my name were singled spaced on the left. It was so plain. I thought it was some legal document, so I read it.

The first line of the letter shook me. It reads:

> "You may not think of yourself as an Angel. But you are."

There was more to the letter, it ended up being from a homeless shelter, however, in that moment, it was an affirmation of where I was, and a confirmation of who I Am.

I see this as a conversation, a connection between Self and Spirit. It is important for us to study these types of happenings in order to understand how Spirit works.

We sway as we learn the language of Spirit. We begin to move from curiosity, to awe. We learn the difference between projecting our desires onto the world, and listening for a course of action. We learn to step back, feel into things, wait, and then act as directed. This is critical for an Angel.

In time we begin to understand we can relax a bit, we will not be sent on assignments we are not ready to handle. If we mess up, we pray and learn. We can be comforted by the fact that Heaven has many ways, and Heaven's will is not thwarted.

*

Forgiveness is another aspect of Swaying. A difficult, and sometimes guilt laden virtue if not understood.

In my growing up years, I felt forgiveness as a sort of giving-in. I understood forgiveness to be giving another a pass, a release from what they had done. I was taught to forgive even when I wasn't ready. He trespassed. "It doesn't matter, you must forgive him." In this type of offering up of forgiveness, there is no resolution. I forgave because this is what I was told was the right thing to do. Jesus told us to forgive. I must do unto others, as I would have them do unto me.

The person who suffers the trespass suffers another trespass when they are not validated, and expected to give to the one who hurt them.

Later, I was told forgiveness was for me. But I truly did not understand how it could be when I felt I was giving it because I was supposed to.

I was told that I must let go, that it was hurting me more to hold onto the trespass. I knew it was hurting me to hold onto it, but I could not let go because I did not feel I had the right to even feel the trespass! I was so conditioned to immediately forgive, that I had to override my own truth to do so.

The Aramaic word for forgiveness means, to cancel, to let loose or to untie.

There are times to cancel. And there are times to let loose, or untie.

When we untie, we release. Releasing is giving back the rope to the one who tied it around us. We do this best energetically, within ourselves. "This is what you have done, I give it back to you." In acknowledging the trespass and saying, this does not belong to me, I feel strengthened. I do not have to hold onto it because it is not mine to hold. It is the trespasser's transgression. I heal myself through my relationship with my, I AM Presence and the Ascended Host. I do not wish them harm. I pray for them because I know the energy they sent will go back to them if they have no care for what they have done.

If they have attended to their Spirit, if they have worked through this trespass with their I AM Presence, or a member of the Ascended Host, their karma will be absorbed. This is in no way a free pass. In the working out of the trespass, they will have acknowledged and seen what they have done. This is no easy task. The sorrow they suffer as a result is what changes them. Humility is a flower of this acknowledgment.

If we hold onto anger because we do not see that they have suffered as a result of what they have done, this is revenge, and it has an energy of it's own. A devouring energy that devours the one whom carries it. Best to allow Heaven to take care of these affairs, and spend time healing our selves, and growing in the Light. Heaven will restore us in many ways.

There are many processes in healing. Acknowledging our pain, feeling our pain, understanding it, and honoring it. When we honor our process and give ourselves the space to heal, we can then move into the aspects of acceptance and letting go. In honoring one's feelings and perceptions, one finds them selves. One individuates and this brings great power.

Swaying is not always painful. We have periods where there are minor mishaps, and periods of deeper growth. It is always our desire for Truth that brings us back to ourselves, and to all Life.

***

FLYING

One may ask, "If there are Angels on Earth, why don't we see their wings?" If you saw an Angel flying through the air right now, it would probably blow your mind.

Angels do not need wings to fly. Wings as we know them on Earth are what the human mind can accept as a manifestation of flying. The logic mind says, in order to fly, one must have wings. Flying to an Angel is all about scaling the dimensions. One does not need wings, or a body to do so. The body manifests as a separate entity when it is needed. It manifests in a way that the dimension can relate to it.

In the beginning of my awakening, I had to give up on obsessive questions and idealizations surrounding the issue of wings. I realized after much deliberation that it was a hindrance on my path.

Living here, we work in the seen and the unseen worlds simultaneously. Much of our flying is centered on moving up the dimensions to speak with the Ascended Host, receiving messages, and delivering messages either in person or telepathically.

Flying through the dimensions is accomplished as an Awakening Angel learns to leave behind the life they believed in, and embraces the Truth of who they are; Beings who are here in order to raise the consciousness of the Souls on Earth. This revelation being grounded in this Truth will give you the wings, and the experience of flight you so long for.

CHAPTER III
THE PLAYING FIELD

When the blind cannot see, it is up to those who do see to help them along their path.

THE FALLEN CONSCIOUSNESS

How did we get here? How did the world get to be in such a state of violence, selfishness, and chaos? This is a very good question. The answer lies in a brief moment in time. If you think on what has been taught about manifestation, you can see that there is a chain reaction to events unfolding. If stacked right, you tip a domino, and it will fall. Fall into the next, into the next, into the next, until they fall to the end of the line. This is exactly what happened in what is known as the Fall of Man.

Currently on Earth we hear the terms, Maya, and illusion. These terms describe the belief that physical manifestation is the supreme reality. Delusion is probably the best word. Believing physical manifestation is the supreme reality is a delusion. Since we cannot see this belief due to it's abstract nature, I often refer to this delusion as an etheric cloud. A cloud that can grow darker depending upon the thoughts that create it. This cloud hovers at the top of the 3rd Dimension and is interwoven with the 4th Dimension. One cannot see these frequencies with the eyes of the physical body. They are known by those who can travel there through meditation, and prayer.

The 4th Dimension acts like a filtering system, so to speak. It houses the negative thoughts of the Collective Consciousness because they are not allowed into the 5th Dimension. This is an important point. These negative thoughts simply cannot rise to the level of the Light of the Fifth, because the level of Light in the Fifth creates a border. The type that sizzles darkness.
The 4th Dimension is also the home for discarnate Spirits. Beings who have etheric bodies, but who are of a low level of Light of varying degrees who may, or may not be able to reincarnate or move on until they reach for the light; and keep reaching.

This dimension is also known as the Astral Plane, and the Emotional Realm. It is known as the Astral Plane because it is non-physical in nature. It is known as the, Emotional Realm, because our emotional energy rises to that level.

According to their emotional intensity, one's thoughts either continue to gather momentum there and move back down into the 3rd Dimension, which then creates its form, or if one's thoughts are of a higher nature, positive and loving, they move through the 4th Dimension into the 5th.

Preferably, the emotional intensity is one of Love and raises higher, coloring itself with a finer more beautiful light from the 5th Dimension. Reaching up into the 5th, and bringing it back down into the 3rd, will bring with it the most power. It is a purer form of Light without distortions, or shadows, and its manifestation will reflect that Light. When you look in that mirror, you will see God.

The 4th Dimensional manifestations will reflect man's egoic thinking because they are of the combined influences of the individual and Collective Consciousness of man living beneath the veil; the cloud. Either way, these emotional thought forms come back down to the Physical Plane as a dense representation of themselves. The mirror.

This is why they say one must pass through the, Angel of the Presence, or the Center Point of the Cross. One must cross linear, horizontal thinking, man's thinking, and move vertically up the dimensions. Learn to bypass the 4th Dimension and reach up into the 5th, Heaven.

There are many hindrances, judgments, desires, attachments, and expectations. They are all something we must master within ourselves if we are to move past the Astral Plane and into the more loving existence of Heaven. Self-ambition is such a hindrance, as well as lack of belief in the self.

As one moves through the 4th Dimension, everything becomes heightened. Fears and worries become exacerbated. A flood of overwhelming thoughts may try to invade one's mind. There may be feelings of confusion and doubt. In this place, in the center of the cross we make a determination. What will be my strongest belief?

Remember, the cloud filters our darkness. It is on the edge of Light.

The dimensions are always merging into each other at the borders, just as any of the frequencies vibrate toward each other. Think of the rainbow. Like attracts like, equally, pushing to exclude unlike itself. The octave between, a double corresponding wave. The space between, navigating two oceans.

Our culture unconsciously refers to this all of the time as the: highs and lows of life whether in feelings, or the money market.

You are either going up,

or you are going down.

As you can now imagine, or perhaps already know, the 4th Dimension becomes a very tricky dimension if you do not understand what is occurring there, nor know how to protect yourself from it.

*

The 3rd is the Dimension of the Lost Souls. Those who are asleep and those who are waking up. They have set up systems which they believe are life. The Angels are here to clear the air, so to speak. As an Angel awakens, we learn to think in more abstract ways. We see life, both spiritually and physically, more objectively than subjectively. Simultaneously, our sensitivity grows. One becomes acutely aware of energy, and can read it's manifested forms.

In the beginning, becoming aware of the various ways darkness manifests itself can be daunting. This is our growth, our moving up into Light. Remember, we have to move through the 4th Dimension. So, if we are untrained in how to move through it, and get stuck there, the mirrored manifestations that are presented can be unfulfilling, unattractive, or downright painful. This is why we must call for the Light. When we call for the Light, it burns away the darkness. First by revealing it. Then, with a conscious letting go, "Yes, I will release this belief". When we let go of the darkness, the Light consumes it.

*

In the Matrix, the Oracle tells Neo, "You've already made the choice. You need to understand *why* you made it."

There is a traditional story in the west, which describes the, Fall of Man. This story being the one of, Adam and Eve. Since I grew up in the west, and am familiar with this story, I would like to break it down for you in order to explain how the fall was manifested, and how an Angel got caught in the mix.

I chose to use the 1611 King James Version of the Bible in this material. It is the 3rd English translation and closer to the common knowledge of those living on Earth today.

Here we go.

Genesis, Chapter 3: 1-24 (1611 King James Version)

I have decided to condense these verses because this version of the Bible is difficult to read, however, please research these verses for yourself, preferably in thee oldest version of the Bible, as you can understand.

Basically, these versus explain that Adam and Eve were in the Garden of Eden, (Heaven) and were told they could eat of any tree except for the Tree of the Knowledge of Good and Evil.

One day, Eve is in the Garden and the crafty serpent comes up to tempt her to eat from the tree. Eve tells him if she eats of the tree, God told her she would die. The serpent tells her she will not die, and the only reason God does not want her to eat of the tree is because he does not want her eyes to be open, nor does he want anyone else to be like him. Eve is convinced and eats the fruit of the tree and offers it to Adam who also eats.

As the story goes, God comes along and confronts Adam, who then blames Eve. Both of them are punished and cast out of the garden, the serpent was punished as well.

This story has been given many literal interpretations, as well as symbolic interpretations. I would like to explain this story at a level many of us have been taught, to one degree or another, in this day and age.

Let us reflect on the laws of manifestation. We do not see our desires, nor how our emotions create. We may see something in our mind's eye, visualizing it, but we do not see it turn into the emotional aspect, we feel that. As our emotions gather momentum, we do not see them project into the atmosphere. Most do not know how this happens, or that it happens. This aspect of manifesting is subtle.

Temptation is crafty. It covers the mind and emotions with desire. It pulls on the consciousness. One has a choice to go this way or that. One choice could seem more desirous than another, even though we may be warned it is not good for us. We may want to try it just because we are curious. However, I do not encourage any unconscious choices.

Never having experienced evil before, Eve did not know what it was. Perhaps Eve was divided within herself and as she contemplated the choice, her emotions grew until they manifested her dominant desire.

Her internal dialogue could go something like this:

"This tree is truly beautiful. I wonder why God doesn't want us to eat from it. He said if we touch it, we will die. Would we really die? He said it was the, Tree of the Knowledge of Good and Evil. What is the knowledge of good and evil? Maybe if we had the knowledge of good and evil, we would be like God. I want knowledge. I want to be like God. God knows what good and evil are. Maybe God doesn't want us to be like him. Maybe he is trying to keep us down. Why can't I be like him? I want to know what good and evil are. I want to be like God!"

Then she eats the apple.

Her actions show what her dominant intension was. She wanted to be like God and experience good and evil. Yet, Eve was already a

Co-creator, made in the image of God.

Genesis 1:27 (1611 King James Version)

27: So God created man in his own image, in the image of God created he him; male and female created he them.

God is pure consciousness, both male and female. Adam and Eve were created in, 'his image'. They are spiritual consciousness, a manifested projection of the male and female aspects of God.

Let's take a look at how Adam and Eve's bodies became infused with Spirit.
Genesis 2:7 (1611 King James Version)

7: And the LORD God formed man of the dust of the ground, and breathed into his nostrils the breath of life; and man became a living soul.

The above passage speaks about how the body and Soul are two different things. There are many questions around when the Soul enters a body, some believe at the moment of conception, others believe after birth. Regardless of when the Soul enters the body; the Soul enters the body. It is the Soul, the consciousness of an individual being that is made in the image of God. When God breathes life into a body, this Soul causes the physical body to become a conscious entity.

When one has consciousness, one is capable of creating, of manifesting.

What is the, Knowledge of Good and Evil, and why didn't God want them to have it? Was it truly because God believed they would be like him and he didn't want that? How could that be if God created them in his own image? Could it be God was trying to warn them?

A common thinking in our world is, you have to know the darkness to appreciate the Light.

Is this true? I believe this to be an excuse from the eons of darkness manifested in the Collective Consciousness. Surely, if we see something bad happen to someone, we will appreciate the fact that it didn't happen to us. This does not mean what happened was necessary. Just because we may sink to the lowest common denominator in our manifesting does not mean we had to in order to appreciate life, or even learn a lesson. It means we sunk to that level because we didn't know what we were doing. Unconsciousness goes down. Consciousness goes up.

Why was the, Tree of Good and Evil in the garden? There is always a choice because there is always Free Will. One is free to experience whatever dimension they like. In manifesting they talk about contrast. Contrast means the opposite of something. I like this I don't like that. I approve of this I disapprove of that. You make a decision, you don't like the outcome, and you make another decision.

Contrast does not have to be evil; it does not have to be painful. I could buy a chocolate ice cream cone, not like it, and go and buy a vanilla.

I guess the question is, how much contrast do you need?

When I have touched the Heart of God, the unspeakable joy I have felt did not convince me I needed to know evil to appreciate the joy. I believe living in evil has clouded our thinking. Contrast does not have to be evil, as the ongoing saga of good vs. evil upon Planet Earth states that it does.

Our Creator knows what evil is. It doesn't say our Creator lives in evil, needs the contrast of evil. Which is why our Creator lives in a higher dimension of Light. Our Creator protected this higher dimension so evil could not dwell in the Garden, the 5th Dimension, the beginning of Heaven. This protection is the filter, the 4th Dimension.

If we continue with the story, we see that God banishes them from the Garden because he does not want them to partake of the Tree of Life and he places Cherubim and a flaming sword, which turns every way to protect the Tree of Life. Genesis 3-23:24 (1611 King James

Version)

God did not literally toss Adam and Eve out of the Garden. The Fall of Man is truly a fall in Consciousness.

Heaven, in and of itself, begins in the 5th Dimension. Lower vibrations simply cannot resonate with it, and will automatically fall lower to the 4th and 3rd Dimensions. Adam and Eve had already decided that they wanted to experience good and evil, and *this* is what catapulted them into the 3rd Dimension.

The 3rd Dimension is a much denser energy; it feels like, 'thee' reality. Forms are tangible; we can pick them up, and move them around. There is a continuity of time; we perceive past, present and future. For many, their attention and desires are predominately 3rd Dimensional based; they believe what is in front of them. Because of this subtle shift in perception, Beings can easily get trapped and continue to create egoic manifestations. Though one may have a sense that something is missing, they may not know what it is, and therefore do not know how to go about filling this void. God was trying to prevent this by warning Adam and Eve.

The resulting punishments that Adam and Eve are said to have suffered, were a result of their separating their consciousness and thus, their vibration lowered into the 3rd Dimension. They were cut off from their Heavenly reality because of what they believed; if they ate of the Tree of Good and Evil, they would surely die. Their beliefs inflicted this punishment, plus, they were young, and they did not fully understand manifestation.

Did Adam and Eve understand what death was? Adam and Eve were young Co-creators. They were learning in the 5th Dimension, Heaven, the Garden of Spirit. The temptation to know things, which they were not ready to handle, caused them to fall in consciousness. Falling into 3rd Dimensional thinking, they were not able to get out from under these manifestations because they blinded them. Biting the apple means going for it, wanting, intending, believing, manifesting. Think about going from a high level of living and then being projected down into a dimension of a much lower consciousness, kind of like if you were suddenly transformed into a dog.

Death as we know it is due to the split in consciousness that occurred as a result of remaining in 3rd Dimensional egoic thinking. Living separately from the 5th Dimension, Heaven, one believes they are merely a body. This belief, as well as living under and partaking in, the illusions in the Collective Consciousness, cause the physical body to break down. The majority of Beings on this planet believe in death. They believe in disease and more aggressive forms of death, murder, and war.

Reincarnation was the result of one not being able to complete their connection to the 5th Dimension before the body gave way. A Being that holds Light simply cannot die in the literal sense. If stuck in lower forms of consciousness, they cannot ascend into the Heavenly Realms, so they are reborn into the state of consciousness they were in at the time of their departure. With a fresh body, the being can begin again, and try to understand the house of mirrors they have put themselves in.

Some teach that karma is the reason for reincarnation. It is not the burning off of old debts that is required. It is the burning off of old beliefs that raises ones consciousness and takes them out of the maze, making them one with their Creator, which then brings Life Everlasting.

Life Everlasting is raising one's consciousness to the point where one understands the difference between egoic thinking and Spiritual Truth. They live Spiritual Truth as their sole reality. Co-creators cannot eat from the Tree of Life; they cannot partake of Heaven, until they raise their consciousness up into the 5th Dimension. This is not a punishment. It is a natural occurrence of one's state of consciousness. This is why the Tibetan says, "Hold your mind steady in the Light".

Reaching the 5th Dimension is possible when one no longer desires ego manifestations to be the basis of reality; when one no longer desires control based upon human logic. When one reaches up to the 5th Dimension, they begin to release their expectations. In time, they learn they can trust because they are connected to Spirit, which reveals itself to them when they seek it. They yearn to know Love, and through this consistent desire, they merge with their Spirit unto full consciousness because it is their final Truth, and there is no other Truth. This level of consciousness is Life Everlasting because there is only one reality, the reality of Life Everlasting. This is the Tree of Life.

*

Throughout the Bible, man is being punished over and over again. This is because of the belief in punishment itself. In the early days, people were under the spell of their belief in Satan. They believed temptations were coming from outside of themselves, from Satan, because they were clueless as to where they were coming from. They had no idea they manifested their own reality. When they experienced the outward form of their own thinking and beliefs, if these forms were negative in nature, they attributed it to God punishing them. The same is true if they manifested positive outcomes, they would say God was blessing them, or rewarding them.

In times past, how could a Co-creator speak, let alone believe, they were made in the image of God? Though it is stated in the Bible, it is never truly explained. It is actually taught that it is one of the biggest sins a human can make, believing they are gods. It is seen as blasphemy. It was the excuse that was given for the killing of Jesus Christ.

Some may ask, Why didn't God just tell them about good and evil?

He did. God warned them not to bite off more than they could chew. Adam and Eve were learning how manifestation works while they were living in the Garden, but they bit off more than they could chew. One could interpret, "if you eat the apple you will surely die" as, "If you follow this line of thinking, your manifestations will overtake you and you will be lost in a sea of forms, which could lead to the death of your consciousness. You could get so lost, you won't even know where you are, or that you are connected to your Creator".

After all, that is what happened.

The moment Eve made her decision; the ego was born and split her consciousness between God and ego. The split that takes us away from our true connection to our Creator because we see the manifestations before us and believe they are the true reality. *This* is egoic thinking. This is also where the warning of believing in false idols comes from. Believing in the exterior rather than the interior.

The knowledge of good and evil is the realization that our creative abilities could take us down a path that could lead to the death of our consciousness if we don't know how to manage our thinking, or understand it's ways.

Temptation itself is not ego based. Temptation is an inherent part of manifesting. It is our entertaining forms of contrast. It is our use of Free Will, which dictates whether we will go one way or another. Up or down.

*

Let's get back to the story of Adam and Eve and talk about the snake.

Genesis 3:13 (1611 King James Version)

And the LORD God said vnto the woman, What is this that thou hast done? And the woman said, The Serpent beguiled me, and I did eate.

At this point, this split in consciousness has occurred and reveals Eve's egoic thinking. She blames her interior dialogue on an outward manifestation. Something outside of me provoked me. The serpent's presence was already a manifestation of Eve's thinking that is why it was there. It is a reflection of her internal dialogue manifest before her.

In Christianity, the serpent has been referred to as a snake, which is actually the form it took after it was punished. Why was the serpent punished if Eve manifested it? You know that phrase, it takes two to tango. The serpent knew what Eve was contemplating, and he took advantage of her naivety.

The snake has a rich history of symbolism which translates across many cultures, as well as, religions. The snake is known to represent guardianship, transformation, Spiritual awakening, and rebirth. It is no wonder the serpent was turned into a snake in the story of Adam and Eve. However, through time, this snake has shed its skin into other facets of manifestation, as we shall soon see.

***

THE TRUTH OF THE ANGELS

One night I found myself in the bookstore where I came across a book entitled, Fallen Angels. Naturally, I was very curious. Fallen Angels seem to be the reason why we are living in such a state of chaos with Lucifer as the gang leader who deceives others in his quest to outshine God.

This book was scary. As I was reading it, even I began to question myself. However, as I continued, I could see through the cracks and crevices. Whenever a writer wants someone to, take their word for it, one needs to be cautious of the real possibility of deception and research the facts for themselves.

There are many ways to spin a topic; this is why we have debates. How do we get down to the Truth? Research the facts thoroughly while praying for wisdom and guidance. Meditate on this wisdom and guidance, and be open to something new. This will lead one to the Truth. It is critical for an Angel to do their homework.

Many believe they have the Truth. However, there are many levels of Truth. There are as many levels of Truth as there are dimensions. What we believe to be true here on Earth is different than what is true in Heaven. One can easily come from an Earth Plane point of view and tell a story, even come up with some literature to back it. However, one must see all sides to discern correctly.

How do we know that Angels exist? The mention of Angels first came about through the Bible. Some believe the Bible is merely a metaphor. What would it be a metaphor of? Some say it is a reflection on life. What life would that be? Man has certainly been trying to answer the meaning of life for some time now. Each coming up with their own definition; something they can live with. Miracles seem to be explained by some as a fanciful imagination or coincidence. That is until one is experienced first hand.

There is nothing on this earth that can factually prove Angels, Miracles, or even God exist. These are something that must be experienced. One can only experience them by being open to them. This is the difference between the 3rd and 5th Dimensions. Heaven does not need to come down and recruit people. Heaven answers the cry of emptiness. However, one must reach up in order to fill that emptiness.

This feeling of emptiness cannot be proven in a factual way, yet it is experienced by many. Those moving through the daily routines of life, even those whose desires are filled beyond measure find there is something missing. This emptiness is what causes one to ask, "What is the meaning of life?"

Science tries to define life for us. Science comes up with all manner of theories and attempts to prove these theories with factual data. Some of it adds up, some of it does not. Science has not discovered the meaning of life. Science will not discover the meaning of life because science attempts to define what has already been manifested. However, manifestation is on going. It is not stagnant, nor will it ever be.

Though we may not be able to prove universal consciousness, we do have many inventors who have stated that they desired a solution to a problem when it just came to them from, out of the blue. Usually when they were in an altered state of consciousness; where they could shut off the mind. There also have been instances where one inventor discovers a solution and across the planet, another inventor has come up with the same or similar solution. How does this happen? Can we prove how it happens? All we can do is notice that it happened. It has happened more than once, and this is something to take into account.

One cannot take another's word for the existence of God, Angels, or Miracles. There is a very specific reason for this. Each of us must come to the Truth for ourselves. We find this Truth when we search for what is missing. We would not feel something was missing; we would not be searching for the meaning of life if we did not believe there was something more, if we did not desire something more.

This desire lives in us specifically because there is something more. We are the ones that have to reach for that something, no one can give it to us.

If we spend our days looking for the answer to life from a 3rd Dimensional point of view, we will not find it. The 3rd Dimension is the realm of egoic manifestation. This is also something one must discover for them selves. Obviously there is much material being written on manifestation. Did this material come to be simply because others are trying to define life to satisfy their emptiness, or did this material come because of Divine Inspiration; perhaps as it did for the inventors?

The only way you're going to know if you're an Angel; well, you already know, you may just be questioning it. The only way to know is by being what you are. Are you a being of pure Light manifest in form? Are you ready to say to the dark energy created by the ego, "You have no power here?" Create miracles because you can? Add Light because that's what you are here for? Are you ready to walk among the Co-creators? You do not have to say anything to anyone. There is no need to explain, nor defend. Are you ready to walk among the Co-creators being who you are? Are you ready to take your power?

The book on Fallen Angels had stated that the fallen Angels are currently in positions of power to purposefully hurt the sons and daughters of God. It is true that the fallen consciousness has created a resonance with Beings who want to be in positions of power; who create all manner of trying to control others. However, those Beings are not Angels, as we shall see.

If we think about manifestation and the Astral Plane as earlier discussed, we can see that the thousands of years of fearful thinking would create a world of anti-peace.

If we believe in good and evil, somebody's got to take on the role. It's going to be those who have a propensity toward selfishness and greed, and the desire for lust and power. They are generally reincarnated Beings who did not reach for the Light in previous incarnations, nor had a desire to. They were quite satisfied with their exterior manifestations and learned to use the power of manifestation to their advantage. Well, to their limited advantage. If they continue on until death, they will move into the Astral Plane and become one of the Beings that try to steal the Light from others, or try to direct their consciousness to inhabit another's body. However, their time is short.

The only reason these Beings have been allowed to continue in their ways is because the majority of the Co-creators are still waking up to the reality of who they are, and what creation is. However, there is too much suffering. And so, the Ascended Host says, "Co-creators are not using their manifesting abilities. They are allowing the unconscious, and the massive dark forms in the Collective Conscious, run the show creating all manner of suffering. They are individually and collectively breaking the Law of Free Will. Send in more Light. Send in the Angels".

There will come a time when the amount of Light on Earth is greater than the amount of darkness. When this happens, those who carry enough Light will rise up and ascend into the 5th Dimension. Those who remain in darkness, their consciousness will stay in a lower dimension. Of course, Heaven will not leave them to suffer their ignorance forever, and will send Light opportunities for those who want them. It is only those who refuse Light that remain in darkness.

Whenever a being deceives or forces another to partake of their agenda, they are breaking the Law of Free Will. It is imperative for a Co-creator, who is made in the image of God, to step up to the plate. The Ascended Host simply will not come down here and take one's hand and lead them to the pearly gates, one must raise their own consciousness. Of course, the Ascended Host is always willing to help. Thank you, Ascended Host.

Now, it is true that there are many perverted teachings roaming around this planet, some of them being around for thousands of years. These teachings have clouded the minds of the Co-creators. We must remember, when Adam and Eve, and they were not the only ones, when Adam and Eve believed in good and evil, when they believed in death, it manifested. It has been manifesting ever since.

This is precisely why there are perverted teachings. It is not because others are necessarily trying to hold people down. It is a circular manifestation of the same belief in good and evil that started from way back when. A perpetuating wheel of, there's no way out.

*

Many Co-creators have fallen under the delusion of Satan and the fallen Angels, and there is always someone to blame. They are brought up in religions that teach them they are not capable of talking with God themselves, nor really taught what to do with the teaching, "the Kingdom of God is within you." Some are accountable because of laziness on their part. They grow comfortable in their life and the pain they suffer is tolerable to one degree or another. They are taught that someone outside of themselves will save them, so they go about life waiting for death to enter Heaven. Some of them are just plain exhausted from living several reincarnations under the cloud of the Collective Consciousness, and have thrown in the towel.

Angels do shift Light in the Collective Consciousness, we do Radiate Light wherever we are, and some Beings simply do not want it. Unfortunate for them because the darker you go, the darker you can go. As frustrating as it can be at times to watch Co-creators choose darkness, we must always, always bring ourselves back to the Truth that they are under an illusion of their own making. Thus, we must pray for them to return to the Light. This does not mean we are subject to their darkness. Remember, we uphold the Light.

We must also remember we are not here alone, the Ascended Host has been sending in Light, and will continue to send in Light. And of course, there are a multitude of Angels. If we need Light, all we have to do is ask.

*

While I was driving home from the bookstore, I continued to pray for the Truth about the fallen Angels. What came to me was a simple question.

Do you believe Source, All That Is, Father-Mother God, Thee Ulmighty, Creator of Heaven and Earth, Creator of all that is seen and unseen, Creator of all of the trees in the forest; all of the rivers and oceans, Creator of animals and man, of stars and galaxies, would be intimidated by Beings that were created by himself?

At that point, the whole situation became laughable.

Now, lets get to the facts about the Truth of the Angels.

When confronted with a choice, Adam and Eve chose. Yet, another was blamed for their choice. Here is where it gets interesting. For, it was not only the Truth of Christ that was manipulated. It was also, the Truth of the Angels. Let us see how this happens.

In the Bible, Eve said the serpent tricked her. Then God condemns the serpent and commands it to crawl on its belly.

Genesis 3-13:14 (1611 King James Version)

13: And the LORD God said unto the woman, What is this that thou hast done? And the woman said, The serpent beguiled me, and I did eat.

14: And the LORD God said unto the serpent, Because thou hast done this, thou art cursed above all cattle, and above every beast of the field; upon thy belly shalt thou go, and the dust shalt thou eat all the days of thy life:

Where is the Angel in this story? There is no Angel in this story.

The connection between the snake, Satan, and Lucifer, the fallen Angel, happened over time as teachers combined common belief with references from the Old and the New Testaments. From that point, it had become a belief that Satan was the serpent that tricked Eve, and that Satan is the devil; Lucifer, a fallen Angel.

The idea that the snake is a supernatural being called Satan or that Satan used the snake, is not something that is literally written in the Bible. The original Hebrew term, satan, is a noun, which was created from a verb, a verb meaning, to obstruct or oppose. Back in the day, anything that would obstruct, or oppose, would be referred to as, satan.

In early Biblical times, Souls on Earth understood the story of Adam and Eve to be literal. They believed the serpent was responsible for tricking Eve. They attributed the serpent to satan. Through time, satan became a being; Satan.

Satan is the evil, which is produced by Co-creators who are ignorant in the use of their power. This projected energy of evil could take on many forms. This energy is referred to as darkness, because darkness obstructs, it opposes the Light.

Through time, Satan turned into Lucifer. It has been said Lucifer was the favorite Angel of God who had fallen because he wanted to be God.

Prior to my understanding of who Lucifer truly is, I had toyed with this common belief. "Hm, why did Lucifer want to be God? Perhaps he was jealous. After all, Angels are servants, maybe he had gotten tired of being ordered around".

I first believed Angels had limited powers. If an Angel wants to be God, they must have limited powers. This is what I have read. Angels have specific gifts; each Angel is assigned to, healing, protection, messenger, or guidance. I realize upon awakening this is not true. Angels are multi-talented. We not only, heal, guide, or protect, we wear many masks, and play many more roles than we are given credit for. We can fly up to the Heart of God, and bring God's Love into many dimensions, which is one of the reasons why we are called messengers. Angels are incredibly powerful Beings, but our true service is to uphold the Light, the Truth of the One. We use our gifts to uphold this Light in service to the One.

Angels were made to live in ongoing oneness with our Creator. Angels are created as conscious Beings. At the same time, our consciousness grows as we continue to expand our Light.

We do not really have the same type of Free Will that a Co-creator has. We can choose. However, we have less of a tendency to choose man's thinking; egoic thinking, because we are so aware of our Creator's thinking. We are so attached to the essence of our Creator that we can see outside of the dimensions. We can look upon them objectively, so we don't really need to choose. We can see what happens. We Love the Light. We were created to Love the Light. We were created to Serve the Light.

We were not created to learn our manifesting skills. We were created to help those who are learning *their* manifesting skills.

Angels on Earth did not fall as man has fallen. Being born on Earth does not make us fallen Angels. We have elected to be here in order to serve. We do have to wake up like everyone else because once we're here in the 3rd dimension, we can get lost even though we do have a stronger connection to Truth which enables us to wake up faster. Above all else, an Angel yearns for the Light.

Our Creator created us this way so we could understand and know the great Love in which we serve, and in that knowing, protect that which is True. We are loyal to our Creator. Not because our Creator can take our life, but because our Creator gave us life and all of the splendor that goes with it.

Remember, an Angel is created as a conscious being that wants to serve our Creator. Because of the way we are created, we do not have a desire to be God. This idea is actually funny to us. We Love who we are. We are conscious Beings of Light!

The reality is it was Adam and Eve that wanted to be like God.

*

Why would the Angels be discredited? Because the Collective Consciousness grew darker over time with fears of evil and punishment there had to be someone to blame. We must remember the Co-creators on Earth are primarily unconscious of their role within the universe; most of them do not know they were made in the image of God, or what that truly means.

Historically, when the Ascended Host is about to move through the darkness of the Collective Consciousness in order to help Co-creators, see the Light, they send Angels. They sent an Angel to announce the births of John the Baptist, and Jesus Christ, as well as, many other times.

In times past, Beings did not have the level of consciousness to understand any of what we are talking about today regarding the Laws of Manifestation. They were too afraid, believing in a punishing God, living in the world of forms. They could not see that they were actually creating their own reality, and Angels were the only other Beings they knew of. They simply did not have the Truth, and so could not take responsibility themselves.

It could also be that the powers that were at that time, those who took on the dark side of the Collective Consciousness, simply did not like the, Bearers of Light, the Angels. The Light always reveals the darkness and if a Co-creator does not want to see them selves, they usually want to, shoot the messenger.

Let's continue.

2nd Corinthians 11:12-14 (1611 King James Version)

12: But what I do, that I will do, that I may cut off occasion from them which desire occasion; that wherein they glory, they may be found even as we.

13: For such are false apostles, deceitful workers, transforming themselves into the apostles of Christ.

14: And no marvel; for Satan himself is transformed into an angel of light.

15: Therefore it is no great thing if his ministers also be transformed as the ministers of righteousness; whose end shall be according to their works.

There are estimated to be five hundred years from the ending of the Old Testament to the beginning of the New Testament. Five hundred years is a long time.

At this time in history, Satan has been personified and is commonly referred to as, Satan, the Angel. Even though there is no passage in the Bible where it is says, Satan is an Angel. What is funny is, this passage actually is the literal truth. Satan was transformed into an Angel of Light. Not because Satan is capable of such a thing, remember Satan was a verb changed into a noun, but because man does not take responsibility for his own creations. That which obstructs the Light, opposes the Light, this is the ego. Not an Angel. False prophets, deceitful workers, these Beings are working through their egos which manifest darkness which obstructs and opposes.

In later times, the Biblical passage of 2nd Corinthians 11:14 was changed to read, *"And no wonder, for Satan himself masquerades as an angel of light"*. This is the common use of the passage in these times.

*

Let's look at how Satan becomes Lucifer.

The passage that many use to link Satan and Lucifer is this one:

Isaiah 14:12 (NRSV)

How you are fallen from heaven, O Day Star, son of Dawn! How you are cut down to the ground, you who laid the nations low!

13: You said in your heart, 'I will ascend to heaven; above the stars of God I will set my throne on high; I will sit on the mount of assembly in the far north;

14: I will ascend above the heights of the clouds, I will make myself like the Most High.'

15: But you are brought down to Sheol, to the depths of the Pit.

16: Those who see you will stare at you, and ponder over you: 'Is this the man who made the earth tremble, who shook kingdoms,

17: who made the world like a desert and overthrew its cities, who did not let his prisoners go home?'

Isaiah asks in 14:16, "...Is this the man who made the earth tremble, who shook the kingdoms," Isaiah does not ask, "Is this the Angel..."

If one reads the story as it leads up to this passage, we see that Isaiah is angry with the King of Babylon due to the king's pride. He is drawing a sarcastic comparison, calling him, Day Star, and son of Dawn. Much like we could sarcastically say to someone who is a dictator, "You Prince of Peace, you Gandhi!" Is the dictator literally, a Prince of Peace? Is the dictator Gandhi?

The name Lucifer means, Morning Star, Day Star, or Dawn. Lucifer is the name of the brightest star in the sky; Venus. In different translations of the Bible, they interchange these words.

Here in a later version of the King James Bible, writers replace Day Star with O Lucifer.

Isaiah 14 (Standard King James Version - Pure Cambridge Edition)

12: How art thou fallen from heaven, O Lucifer, son of the morning! how art thou cut down to the ground, which didst weaken the nations!

13: For thou has said in thine heart, I will ascend into heaven, I will exalt my thrown above the stars of God: I will sit also upon the mount of the congregation, in the sides of the north;

14: I will ascend above the heights of the clouds; I will be like the most High.

15: Yet thou shalt be brought down to hell, to the sides of the pit.

16: They that see thee shall narrowly look upon thee, and consider thee, saying, Is this the man that made the earth to tremble, that did shake kingdoms;

17: That made the world as a wilderness, and destroyed the cities thereof; that opened not the house of his prisoners?

18: All the kings of the nations, even all of them, lie in glory, every one in his own house.

Through reading early interpretations of the Bible, one can see how meanings can be changed over time. However there was something that was not changed over time. Even in this edition Isaiah asks, "Is this the man..." He does not ask, "Is this the Angel?"

*

Here is another common passage that is used to refer to Lucifer, the fallen Angel:

Ephesians 2:2 (1611 King James Version)

Wherein in time past ye walked according to the course of this world, according to the prince of the power of the air, the spirit that now worketh in the children of disobedience:

Paul is referring to those walking according to the ways of the world. Those who are ignorant of their true Spiritual heritage, and thus through egoic beliefs, create destruction out of a desire to control.

Those who interpret the Bible literally translate 'the prince of the power of the air' as Lucifer, the fallen Angel. The only Beings they knew of that fly are Angels.

In actuality, the 'prince of the power of the air' refers to the evil living in the Collective Consciousness, the unseen cloud above our heads. The 4th Dimension, the Astral Plane. These planes are given the identity of a prince because the power of these thought forms have a tendency to lead people, to govern them when they do not govern themselves. This is the automatic pilot aspect of the Collective Consciousness. Whatever holds sway in the Collective Consciousness manifests on Earth.

*

Here is another New Testament passage that gets used a lot to refer to what now has grown into a gang of fallen Angels. The Powers and Principalities -- in high places.

Ephesians 6:12 (King James Bible, Cambridge Edition)

For we wrestle not against flesh and blood, but against principalities, against powers, against the rulers of the darkness of this world, against spiritual wickedness in high places.

It would make sense in terms of manifestation that the belief in evil would eventually create a manifestation of that evil. The laws of manifestation do not necessarily dictate a specific physical manifestation, but the manifestation of the essence of the belief. The essence.

Some would argue. No, I wanted a red BMW with air conditioning and a great stereo and I got one!

Yes, you could do that. But I am talking about a general belief. The belief in evil. It could manifest in many ways.

The Powers, are the powers of the emotions, the intentions. The Principalities, are the principals of manifestation. This is why he says we wrestle not against flesh and blood. We wrestle against the energy, the negative beliefs which create forms like themselves. He refers to the rulers of darkness of this world, against spiritual wickedness in high places, the rulers that use the knowledge of manifestation to their advantage. That continue to create the cloud. The bigger it gets the darker it gets the more control they have.

All of us wrestle with this and Angels do the most because we see it more.

*

I hope I have been able to shine the Light on the fact that Lucifer is not a fallen Angel, nor is he satan. Satan is not a being, but a manifestation of darkness overall, and that the only ones who wanted to be gods were Adam and Eve. Eve, in her inability to understand her own manifestations, and through her own feelings of shame and guilt manifested such.

"Don't let one bad apple spoil the whole bunch, girl." -- Jackson

Five

I will now tell you how thee dark forces operate in this plane. They convince you that form is reality, that you are your body and must be a religious slave, and give your attentions to the world that you see, and wait many lifetimes before you could even begin to live in truth, they teach this in many religions. Adam was not punished, he dropped into lower levels of consciousness and thus reaped the consequence of that consciousness. It could be interpreted as punishment, but that is through a lack of understanding. For we are taught they were severely punished.

We were taught they had no free will in the garden. That is not true. We were created with free will, regardless of what dimension we are in. They were taught that God commanded them to not eat of the fruit. Why would God command if he has given free will? I believe he would warn, and I believe he did warn, and many times sent Light to his angels, and those who are lost.

***

THE SUNS OF GOD

When God created Co-creators, he projected his consciousness, which is thee highest Light, which then takes form. God created Co-creators in Heaven. Their forms were different, much more etheric in nature. The lower one goes in the dimensions, the denser that form will be.

Co-creators, those made in the image and likeness of God, were created like a sun. A small sun. So many in the fields of Energy Healing speak of the Core Star. It is a core of Light within us that we can connect to and expand. This Core Star is a point of Light midway between the third and forth chakras. When we are connected to it, it opens the chakras and the fullness of our Light can shine forth.

This is our Spiritual Essence. From this point we project our Spiritual Consciousness through our energetic bodies. We are here. We are present. From this place, we can Direct the Light.

The Core Star is activated when we come from our Will. Right Use of Will is the goal; anything less than a connection to Spirit will not bring the results one is looking for. Right Use of Will is being connected to our Spiritual Essence and moving into the world from its perspective. When we are one with our Spiritual Essence, we are Conscious and can move in the world in Conscious ways.

Holding Full Consciousness takes time. Full Consciousness in physical form takes practice. This is a lot of Light, and some people can't handle the intensity of it. It is Power. Consciously Directed Will is Power. Right Use of Power is Divine. Claim your Light. Yes, it can be difficult because the world is not used to it. But how will the world shift if we do not do this?

*

Co-creators are manifest Beings of the Light. They were not born as God. Co-creators have their own identity, with similar abilities as our Creator. One of these being the ability to create, to manifest. This, as a newly created Being of Light, is what they must learn.

If Co-creators are the, Suns of God, it would make sense that as the Light extends, it is extending into the void, into the darkness. It is when one looks upon the darkness and fears it does the darkness have control. For if one turned to the Light, saw one was made of Light, then one would have no fear of darkness. We all know that Light consumes the darkness.

What creates? Consciousness creates. Consciousness creates like itself it projects. It projects what it believes.

Do you believe in darkness? In my Fathers house there are many mansions. Those who believe in the darkness, live in the darkness.

The Light of God is forever expanding. Angels carry that Light. We come in our Light so Co-creators can see in the dark. We may be considered at times, the Light at the end of the tunnel.

*

Round and round and round we go, when we'll stop, nobody knows.

Free Will.

Take a bite of the Big Apple. See and do it all!

The question becomes, do you like what you're manifesting?

With Free Will comes choice. One can expand into the Light, or contract into the darkness.

Co-creators are making choices every day. The problem has been, even with the teachings on manifesting, they are not aware of the extent of this. They are blinded by their perceptions because they have created a very large, very complex, house of mirrors.

This house of mirrors is starting to crumble. There is a deep level of suffering on this planet. A suffering that does not seem to truly penetrate the inner fibers of some Beings. War. Famine. Abuse. Poverty. We are afraid of these things. They hurt us in individual ways. In this sorrow is a cry. Not always aloud, but in our Hearts. This cry is heard through the Heavens, "We are lost. We have lost our way. We hurt, but we don't know why we hurt, and we don't really know what to do".

The teachings on manifesting have come at a very good time. However, some of those teachings are geared toward artificial aims, and pulling some farther off the path. Many understand manifestation as merely a tool to get what they desire. They are taught that they came here specifically to experience the 3rd Dimension. When one believes they came here to, play around, one does not often think of how to use the Laws of Manifesting to climb into the higher dimensions. They often do not seek to know how the Collective Consciousness manifests, or even how life on Planet Earth came to be as a result of it. This teaching can keep a being blinded and bound to the 3rd Dimension.

The problem and the solution is the shift in individual consciousness which then expands into the Collective Consciousness.
The Collective Consciousness exists. We are made of consciousness and together we share in a group consciousness. Not being aware of this, Co-creators have created all manner of ways to keep themselves behind the veil. Dogmatic Religions; Dictators; Materialism. Systems of control and excess are all created out of fear.

Please understand this is not a teaching against any government or religion. If we truly understand manifestation, we will see these are manifestations of collected beliefs. And they change over time as Co-creators change over time.

If we go back to the teachings of the Astral Plane, the 4th Dimension, we will remember that this plane holds the pre-manifested states of the Collective Consciousness. In ignorance it has grown dark and attracts like itself. It becomes the home of incarnate Beings who attach themselves to that plane and are available for all who would agree with them. As the thought forms grow in intensity, i.e., selfishness, lust, expectation, revenge, etc., the energy of these discarnate Beings can move into a willing participant. This is the talk of evil spirits and demons. Dictators portray our belief that we can be oppressed. They say, "The Light can be shut off!"

Co-creators who do not know their own power, who do not know they are made in the image of our Creator, have a good chance being influenced by the 4th Dimension and the Beings in it. Unconscious Co-creators decide for themselves what is right and what is wrong, and voila, here we are! To the degree one is willing to look at themselves and the results of their behavior, their manifestations, is to the degree one is able to touch the Light within. If one steps away from that opportunity, one can grow increasingly darker. Choices. The dominos have fallen and their path has lead to darkness.

When Christ said to live in the world and be not of the world, he was talking about taking the fork out of the road. There is no other road, no other world. There is only one world, Spiritual Consciousness. Hell is of one's own making. Or, a collective hell if one wants to join that group.

How do we walk this one road while living in the 3rd Dimension? By understanding the 3rd Dimension is made of form, easily changeable by consciousness. We understand that consciousness creates and this is all we need to know. We say, what I see before me can shift; there is no darkness in the Light. We do not give the darkness any power.

The Suns of God were made to shine. Angels are here to ignite them.

THE COLLECTIVE CONSCIOUSNESS

What happens when a group of Co-creators create? Since the Laws of Manifestation are based on the focus of conscious energy, whatever is believed will be manifest in form. When many Co-creators believe in the same things, over and over again, and give their emotions to these beliefs, the more these beliefs manifest in our world. We see this all the time as the reflections of our collective thinking are revealed through our television shows, movies, music, advertising, news reports, politics, fashion, racism, wars.

If you are living on Planet Earth you are affected by the Collective Consciousness. It is the mass accumulation of our thoughts and beliefs. The majority of these beliefs are based upon division. Who has what? Who is better looking, who is more successful? Who is a horrible person? Who deserves to live? Who deserves to die? And on and on. All comparisons are based on duality thinking.

The Duality Consciousness is total ego consciousness split off from God. The ego dictates what is good and what is bad based on it's three dimensional thinking; making judgments based on it's own point of view. All of the ego's thinking is based upon the belief in form, i.e., one has a body, one needs to provide for the body; these are the ways that one can provide for the body, the types of careers, lifestyles, and all manner of choices that distract oneself from their Soul.

In the Heavenly Realms, there is only one consciousness, the consciousness of Light. This is why Masters tell us to go within, refer to the Light within, the Kingdom of God, within.

Some teach one chooses to come to Earth to have a specific experience of a pre-defined choosing in order for one's Spirit to grow. Growth does come from being here. As we learn what we are attracting into our field of Self, we learn how to choose wisely.

However, to believe one purposefully comes here to specifically do this, can lock one into believing they must continue to come here in order to grow. This is the 3rd Dimension. It is one of the lowest dimensions there are. A Being made in the image of God does not need to come here in order to grow. A Spiritual Being is here because they are unconscious, hopefully, growing in consciousness. There are all manner of experiences, choices, and growth in the 5th Dimension and beyond. There are Ascended Masters, and then there are, Ascended Masters.

Of course, all have Free Will. If one wanted to descend into the 3rd Dimension to have a type of experience, well, buckle your seat belt. You will lose a large portion of your consciousness and you will not be able to ascend into higher dimensions until you master the 3rd. Most cannot come into the 3rd Dimension as a fully conscious being. The vibration is too low for that.

When one comes here, their consciousness is affected by the Collective Consciousness, which radiates a very powerful delusion that the 3rd Dimension is, Reality. Those who master this level and move up into the 5th Dimension have better things to do than come back down; most of them are working on moving up into higher dimensions. Those who come here holding more Light have volunteered to come here, and they must also work their way up. However, it is easier for them, and in so doing, they add Light into the Collective Consciousness and teach others along the way.

Others teach we are gods at play losing ourselves in the lower realms in order to be, the pauper, the entertainer, the priest, the prophet. I wonder if those who are starving, or being blown apart by war, are enjoying their experience in form. I'm wondering what they are learning. How cruel life can be? Perhaps they should have picked another role. Some would call this karma.

I wonder while they are starving if they are aware that they are paying a debt. Perhaps while they are lying there suffering a horrific death their past life plays before them, and they see where they have starved another and come to peace saying, 'Yes, I know what I have done. My debt is paid.' What of the man who is suddenly shot to death, where is his moment of remembrance?

It is true we learn compassion when something we have done to another happens to us. Is this a debt we are paying, or is it an expansion of our consciousness? It is an expansion of our consciousness. We feel sorrow for what we have done, and learn a deeper compassion, which brings Light into the world. We all fall. Believing we must pay our debt in the same way we created it is a belief in punishment. We raise our consciousness by our desire to Love. We fall in consciousness when we become selfish and filled with ego desire. We will always experience the effects of our consciousness. If we are vibrating in a low state of consciousness we will attract a low state of consciousness, the same if we are vibrating higher.

Perhaps those who die of starvation are vibrating at a very low level of light. Perhaps they do not know how to raise their level of light. Maybe they are here because collectively, we believe in suffering, and these Beings volunteered to show us who we are; to show us what we believe.

*

Our Creator and the Ascended Host are always sending Beings here with more and more teachings, and more and more Light. This is what the Harmonic Convergence was about. If you look back to the mid-eighties, you will see that there has been a rise in the amount of metaphysical teachings in the world. These teachings have been around before that, but they were harder to come by. There was much more of a belief in going to hell than there is today. This, in and of itself, is a perfect example of the way the Collective Consciousness works.

*

There is another belief roaming about which promotes, "There are no new ideas". Just how many of your thoughts are original? This is not because there are no original thoughts, or ideas. It's because you have been told there are a limited number of thoughts and a limited number of ideas.

Begin to track your thinking. Question it. Ask yourself if you truly believe some of the things you hear, and why you believe them. Jot them down. In time you will see a long list of beliefs that you have learned growing up, not that you came up with on your own.

The apple doesn't fall far from the tree.
You live then you die.
Nothing is guaranteed except death and taxes.
I hate Mondays.
Another day, another dollar.
Thank God it's Friday!
It's their fault! Those (race/politicians/etc.) are the ones who did this!

And because you saw these beliefs played out in front of you, well, of course you believe them. There they are! We have been taught that physical life is reality. Only now are we beginning to learn the Truths of manifestation.

This is also why there is so much talk on ascension. Ascension does not only mean disappearing from the planet because one mastered their ego, it is also ascending from any lower level thinking, to any higher level thinking, or Spiritual Truth.

When I was first learning about ascension I became overwhelmed, "When am I ever going to get out of here!?" Then it came to me that I came here to serve, not to escape. This shifted things dramatically because I felt my sense of purpose, and it made it easier for me to give up not only the desire to escape, but also the many other desires I had to have a different life upon this planet. What I have learned is, although Angels can manifest, they must manifest according to their purpose otherwise it throws everything off and they will be very disappointed. Not only with the outcome, but they will lose a very sacred part of themselves and feel ashamed for serving themselves instead of the One. This can bring deep sorrow to an Angel.

There are various prayers, chants, and mantras that are specifically designed to raise your vibration; raise your conscious awareness. Using these tools will help you gain a broader perspective of who you are and what you believe about life. Since they are accessing higher frequencies of Light, whatever darkness you hold within will be revealed. Question your beliefs and ask for Divine Guidance to let go of any false beliefs about yourself and life.

If you want to live in Love, if you truly want to live in Love, you will be shown the way that is right for you. This is why they say there are many paths, because you are an individual identity with a specific personality, ideas and beliefs. So, there will be some teachings that are better suited for you than others, and these may change over time. One might find them selves studying Buddhism and then a year later they may take to, The Course in Miracles. This is the way. We get moved around according to our level of consciousness.

The good news, because you are part of a collective whole, the thoughts and beliefs you begin to shift will add Light to the darkness in the Collective Consciousness. The more positive and loving thoughts that are interjected into the Collective Consciousness the faster the manifestations on the planet will turn to reflect those thoughts.

Love holds a far greater power than anti-love. Just as a light is turned on in a room, it spreads to the outer edges of darkness, this is exactly what can, and is happening in the Collective Conscious on Earth.

***

A CONVERSATION WITH THE ASCENDED HOST AND THE FORCES OF DARKNESS

The following is a conversation I had with the Ascended Host regarding Free Will. During this time, I was calling for more Light to raise the consciousness on Planet Earth. The Dark Forces (D.F.), the Dark Voices within the Collective Consciousness, were giving me reasons why I could not do this. Their defense being that I would be stepping on another's Free Will.

Through this conversation, you will see how thick, how deeply steeped, the Collective Consciousness is in the darkness, and how it defends itself, always with the same thinking. These voices are the collected beliefs of those past and present that have contributed to the creation of the veil, the cloud in the 3rd and 4th Dimensions.

THE LAW OF FREE WILL: No one in Heaven can prevent another's Free Will. Beings must be the ones to choose between living in the Light or the darkness.

TAMARA: I use your words, Mary. "How can the Souls on Earth make a choice when they do not see a choice?" Therefore, herein is the solution: Penetrate the darkness with Light. The Dark Forces in the Collective Consciousness are only energy, which must transform.

D.F.: Oh, you think you can simply override the Free Will of those who created manifestation according to their liking?

TAMARA: To their liking? They don't even know what they are doing.

D.F.: How can you say that? They seem to be enjoying themselves. After all, isn't that why they entered the 3rd Dimension, they wanted to know what evil was?

TAMARA: They entered the 3rd Dimension out of ignorance, not out of a clear conscious choice.

D.F.: Oh, they chose, and you know they chose.

TAMARA: They do not know the Truth of their power. They did not know what evil was. How could they make a clear choice when they don't even know what the choice really is?

D.F.: They are learning. They are being taught about manifestation.

TAMARA: Ah, yes. And they are creating more of the same. Are they teaching manifest your way to Heaven? Aye, some, and thank God!

D.F.: It does not matter the form of the Light, for it is Light. What's your rush?

TAMARA: Can you not hear the cries?

D.F.: Right, and this is where they get to choose. Do they love it here, or do they love it there?

TAMARA: If Souls only see forms before them, they create more forms. These forms do not fill them, because the 3rd Dimension *is* a low level of vibration, they do not realize their Soul is seeking to satisfy its need for Light.

D.F.: It is their choice. They have Free Will.

TAMARA: There are also some who are using their Free Will to overpower another's Free Will.

D.F.: Well, it is up to those who are being overpowered to do something about it.

TAMARA: How can they do something about it when they don't even know it's happening? This is like an endless loop and Souls on Earth are suffering!

D.F.: You're just trying to be God, a typical Angel.

TAMARA: You house untruth, and untruth about the Angels. This endless struggle of good vs. evil winning through pain, and suffering. There always seems to be another tormentor. Another war, another justification. They choose. Ha! Step into the Light and show yourself, doesn't the darkness have to do this?

D.F.: (No Reply)

TAMARA: The Light has the right to reveal the darkness. The darkness must stand and be revealed, or it is consumed by its own darkness. It wants to survive. Through the power of the Collective Consciousness, it has turned into a beast. A vast thought form with a mind of its own pulling and tugging on the minds of Co-creators. And because it is a thought form, and not a spirit of God, which has Free Will, it CAN be destroyed, and by whomever can destroy it! It does not have the right to say, "I exist, therefore, I AM".

A bell is rung and the Assembly grows quiet. After a moment, murmuring begins.

MARY: I agree. Something must be done. The Co-creators simply are lost in their own creations and the situation is only growing darker.

D.F.: I disagree. You want to take away their Free Will.

TAMARA: Think on this: When the sun shines, there are no shadows, only those that rest upon the edges, but we can see those. We can see through them. When we see the shadows, we have Free Will.

D.F.: Are we forgetting it was their choice to experience this? And now you say because of their Free Will choice, they must be saved from it? That is overriding the Law of Free Will.

SPEAKER: Commanding the darkness is not overriding one's Free Will.

D.F.: Yes it is. This is their lesson even if it leads to destruction.

ASSEMBLY MEMBER: If this magnitude of destruction happens, it can shock these Souls, and scatter their consciousness, and destroy Earth.

TAMARA: No! They need more Light! These Souls are locked in systems of beliefs that keep them blind.

D.F.: Do we not have the cycle of birth and death?

TAMARA: The cycle of birth and death is a result of this whole thing that you created with some of your religions. You always want to play the game, the chess game, you always give a little light back with a little darkness mixed in. Keep on going, keep moving forward, it is always darkest before the dawn and on and on.

D.F.: Which originated with the Co-creators.

TAMARA: Yes, who did not know what they were doing. Which is why they need more Light, to see and understand what they are doing. This is how they will truly learn their manifesting skills.

D.F.: I disagree. Our universe--which lives in a darkness--shows the cycles of birth and death, darkness and light.

TAMARA: There is a difference between the darkness of night and the darkness of ignorance.

D.F.: Upon Earth, they see them as the same. Ying and Yang.

TAMARA: Now you know that was perverted into a form of egoic thinking. Stating there must be darkness to appreciate the Light.

D.F.: How can you say that when everyone believes it?

MARY: We of the Ascended Host do not believe it. Which is why we are here and not there.

D.F.: That was your choice.

MARY: A choice that was made from understanding Truth.

TAMARA: Are you saying they must stay there until they learn true evil? To have their Souls devoured by the darkness? So they don't even know who they are? How can they choose then?

D.F.: They have a choice. Even dictators have a choice. There is always a moment, and they let the moment pass.

TAMARA: Do you believe they would have let that moment pass had they known what was really going on? That their desire to oppress was based completely on fear? That they were being tormented by the pull of the darkness inside of the Collective Consciousness, which had been overtaken with fear and hatred?

D.F.: You can't blame a discarnate being, or the Collective Consciousness. If a Soul doesn't want any part of it, they could have fought it off. There are many on Earth who believe dictators have complete Free Will. They have their moment of choice.

TAMARA: But what of the moment of choice for their victims? Are you saying they are both consciously aware of what they are doing?

D.F.: Yes. Each chooses to experience what they want to experience.

TAMARA: No, which is why the word victim is used, the entire act is seen as unholy. One who does not know how to command the Light, the meek, the weak, the down trodden. They already carry the whispers of a tormentor; they already have a shadow following them, some, a demon. They are taught that they are horrible sinners who must accept their punishment, or that they must come back in another life to live their karma.

D.F.: It is only an experience. What are you getting all bent out of shape about?

TAMARA: We would not be having a meeting in the Great Assembly of the Heavenly Realms if this were not a serious matter.

D.F.: I have a right to exist. They have Free Will, and they have chosen me.

TAMARA: Is this about you?

D.F.: It's all about me.

The bell rings and the Assembly takes a break. After a long deliberation and much objection by the Dark Forces in the Collective Conscious, it is decided that more Light will be sent to Earth.

THE DECISION IS READ:

The Law of Free Will states it is up to each and every member of creation to choose life or death for them selves. However, it is agreed that at this time, there is too much darkness in the Collective Consciousness for Souls to see they have a choice. The Council agrees, in order for them to choose freely, they must know what they are choosing and why.

With a slam of the gavel, the meeting was over, and those in charge of sending more Light began to gather together and begin their work.

***

CHAPTER IV

ANGELIC PRAYERS

*In all they do, Angels are drawn to the Light.
Drawn to bring the Light out in others,
and drawn to bring the Light down to Earth.*

THE ENTRANCEWAY OF THE HEART

When we pray, we pray with our hearts. We do not need to speak these prayers out loud, we can speak love internally and say what is true for us to say, it is the sincere vibration of your love that reaches God.

Father God, my father, how I love you and thank you for giving me true life, forgive me for what I have done, I realize _____. I send my love to _____, I send them a blessing of Light, that their troubles will be diminished and they will see you in all things.

***

CALLING AND CLAIMING ONE'S ANGELIC I AM PRESENCE

In the name of My Father who art in Heaven, I call forth the Light and Truth of Love and all that is Holy. I call forth and Claim my Angelic I AM Presence. I hold to my Presence as the True Source of my Life. I am willing to leave behind all egoic lies and desires in order to embrace the Truth of who I AM in the Light.

I AM CREATED AS (Angelic name) THEREFORE I EXIST.
I AM CREATED AS (Angelic name) THEREFORE I EXIST.
I AM CREATED AS (Angelic name) THEREFORE I EXIST.

I am an Angel. A High Being of Light created to serve my Creator and the Heavenly Realms. Created to serve the One and the Many.

I Claim my Angelic Heritage and I Bless all Life.

I Call Forth the Light to fill me, and I accept this Light as the Truth of my Life.

I Call Forth Protection from the Heavenly Realms, and the Angelic Kingdoms.

I Call Forth the White Light of Truth to clear my Aura and my energetic bodies.

I call forth Wisdom and Guidance that I may serve through the portal of my Heart and be a Blessing to all that is True.

Blessed is our Creator, our Love, the Most High.
Blessed be the Angels who serve Love and Light.
Amen and Amen.

***

GRATITUDE

Heavenly Father, I send you my life, I give you all of my heart. Thank you for wanting me. Thank you for giving me existence that I may see your glory of creation, and experience the many miracles and awes of your Light. Bless you Heavenly Father and your Kingdom of Light. (Now extend the love and light from your heart to Heavenly Father).

***

DISCERNMENT AND WISDOM

Father-Mother God, I bring myself before you, asking for a Blessing of your Divine Wisdom. Open my eyes to see Truth. Guide me to the Open Fields.
Pour your Light upon me that I may see and not be afraid. Pour your Light upon me and let Wisdom Shine through my body. Pour your Light upon me; let Wisdom Reign.

Bless you and thank you, Ulmighty God.

Amen and Amen.

***

PRAYER OF SELF-ACCEPTANCE

Feeling depressed, and not able to achieve my goals, I realize I must accept. Accept that there is a plan, a place, and a time that is right. Angels, help me understand that my pushing life keeps it from me.

Angels, help me to see that I am the perfect light I was created to be and will be more as I listen, and learn to trust my inner connection to my father who conceived me.

Help me release the tension I feel, the expectations I hold.

Help me see things unfolding in perfect divinity.

Thank you, my Father, bless you, Holy Angels.

HEALING ANGER

Heavenly Father, oh, Holy Angels help me. I am so angry, please help me trust that you will help me in my troubles. That no person, place or situation is bigger than you, that you will provide for me, that you will defend me, to give me strength and protection, for I know your will is right for me and I trust you will not leave me abandoned. Thank you, Father.

***

PROTECTION

Holy Angels, please protect me, surround me with your presence and help me to see my way. Thank you, Holy Angels.

***

MARY'S HEART FOR A PEACEFUL HOME

I call upon the Pink Heart Light of Mary.

I ask that you enter and bless our home with your gentle kiss of Love. Radiate your Light and sooth the edges; bring healing to the secret places. May our hearts be open to receive your love and strength.

I bless you for your Presence Mary, accept this gift of my Love.

(Take a moment to express your inner gratitude)

I seal this prayer in the Golden White Light of the Heavens. Thank you. Amen & Amen.

CHAPTER V

EMBRACING THE TREE OF LIFE

A Story

Deep in the mists of the forest, there is but one road before me. It leads to a majestic land, of which I cannot see. I take my first step, and become enveloped in shadow. I turn back, but the road has disappeared. I have no choice but to move forward, though it scares me.

The road was uneven, filled with broken glass. I cut myself and bled.

Upon occasion, I would turn back though the road was covered in thick brush. I decided to try to cut my way through, as thorny and as thick as it was. Exhausted and getting nowhere, I decided to press forward, and continue to head for the Majestic Land.

Through grey skies and cold nights, I made my way. I had traveled this road through its twists and turns, and at times I had forgotten where I was going. Then I would remember, but still had to climb those twists and turns. And it seemed when I was about to give up; there was a reason to keep on going.

But this day, this hour, I was ready to give up for good. I stopped to brush the dust from my pants when I looked off to the left. There in the distance, was a city. I was relieved. Deciding I would end my search, I would rest there where I would no longer be alone, and could find some food and shelter.

Farmers and merchants sold their wares at the city gates. It seemed all I could want was there and more. Among them were mothers with their children playing as they were purchasing food, I saw the wise men walking, talking, nodding and shaking their heads. At the end of the city was a palace with high gates. Suddenly trumpets were heard and the city grew quiet.

The gates opened and a procession of wealthy men and women began to move forward. All of the townspeople were in awe of their garments and trinkets. Some of them made of gold, others of diamonds and silk. As they made their way through the city, I notice a small boy looking out at the forest. His mother tried to keep him focused but could not. He slipped from her grasp and starts running. He shouts, "A deer! A deer!"

All of the town looks into the distance, and sees the most stunning silver deer. So beautiful was she, shining in glory and looking back at the people. As the boy approached her, she disappeared with him and the city broke out in aghast.

For days countrymen and city officials searched far and wide for the boy and the deer, but could not find him. His mother in tears, I promised her I would search until the end of time. She thanked me, and I went on my way.

The forest gave way to an expanse of mountains. I had no choice but to climb. Over sharp rocks, and terrifying heights I made my way. I would stop every now and again and eat whatever I could find, sleep where I felt safe.

What propelled me on this road, I wondered. Yet, I realized there was no going back.

And then, there I was on top of the mountain where I saw the Majestic Land deep in the mists. It wouldn't be long now. I must stop and rest. While resting, I had a dream. I was already in the Majestic Land, and there was the boy, and the silver deer. I said to the boy, "Your mother is worried. She wants you home, safe and sound." The boy laughed and said, "I am home, don't you recognize it?" I didn't understand and suddenly awoke.
There before me was the silver deer. She lowered herself so I could climb on top of her. "Where are you taking me?" I asked. She did not respond.
For many miles she moved through the mists. As she walked, I could enjoy the crystalline clouds and a deep sense of peace filled my body. Soon, we were at the entrance and she stopped, and I got off.

The silver deer turned to me and said, "Do you remember your journey? The journey of broken glass, and jagged rocks?"

"Yes, I said. How can I forget it?"

"Here, in this place, it will be no more. Are you ready to let this memory go?"

"Yes," I said. "Of course!"

"I must warn you. If you remember it, even a bit. If you entertain it and roll it around in your mind, you will find yourself back outside of these gates, and there is no telling how far you will have gone."

"Oh, I do not want to remember broken glass and jagged rocks. No worries there." I exclaimed.

Suddenly, the gates to the Majestic Land opened. In the courtyard was a beautiful tree. The silver deer lead me to it and she said, "This is the Tree of Life. You have embraced it and now you are welcome in the Majestic Kingdom."

"Why, I don't remember embracing it." I said.

"Oh, you did. The moment you released the broken glass."

I turned to look back at the road we traveled; the gates still open a wedge. There was nothing there that I wanted. I turned to the tree and embraced it, wrapping my arms around it, and as I did, showers of light fell from its leaves and sparkled upon my body. It was there I was transformed and became the boy.

***

CLOSING THOUGHTS

There are many paths to service and it is up to the Awakening Angel to earnestly grow in understanding the reality that is taking place on this earth from a spiritual perspective, and then realize their part in it.

There has been much teaching that has taken place through these pages, and many tools have been given. One may not understand something today, only to find they understand it tomorrow. Be gentle with yourself in learning this material.

> Call upon the Heavenly Realms to guide you to bring you Revelation.

••

(END OF PART I)

ANGELS ON EARTH

A GUIDE FOR AWAKENING ANGELS

Part II

Tamara of the Angels
Channeled by Bunny Lang

*Did you hear the sound? The clang of the bell?
When it rang, the Angels answered
and Light streamed down from the Heavens.*

A Note and a Blessing

Now we are heading into learning about the powers of energy; how to use it in responsible ways, to heal ourselves and others, to protect ourselves and others and to hear the messages from Holy Spirit whom wishes to move through us.

I pray this guide blesses you in many ways.

Tamara of the Angels

TABLE OF CONTENTS
PART II

DEFINITIONS	127.
CHAPTER I	133.
BODIES OF LIGHT	
Layers of Communication	135.
Your Point of Light	151.
CHAPTER II	155.
LIVING BETWEEN THE WORLDS	
Introduction	157.
Spiritual Discernment	161.
Mighty Messengers	167.
Invoking the Light	177.
Stepping Down the Light	181.
Anchoring the Light	183.
Wielder of the Light	185.
Showers of Light	191.
The Healing of Others	195.
Responsible Manifesting	201.
CHAPTER III	205.
ANGELIC PRAYERS	
Calling and Claiming One's Angelic I AM Presence	209.
The Entranceway to the Heart	211.
Discernment and Wisdom	212.
Desire to Forgive	213
Dissolving Fear	214.
Releasing Expectations & Acceptance	215
Removing Dark Energies	216.
Protection	217.
Mary's Heart Prayer for a Peaceful Home	218.

CHAPTER IV 219.
THE LITTLE GLASS MERMAID (a story)

DEFINITIONS

Why do we use interchangeable words? Throughout history there have been many teachers, Masters, and writers from various cultures, each of them translating their understanding of the universal energies and truths for the time they've lived in. These teachings have been passed around, rewritten, some words used here, and other's there. By studying several religions, teachings, and through meditation and reflection, one learns these words are similar in meaning. I will be referencing the realms in the ways I have come to know them.

Those of us who travel the dimensions receive information at the level we can understand and interpret it. The Heavenly Realms do not use the languages of Earth. They send a ray of Light, a thought form, into the 3rd Dimension. We decode it according to our abilities. Things can get confused in the mix at times. What I do know is this: if you want the Truth, you shall have it.

In this material, I will be teaching about the first five dimensions because that is what is needed at this time.

Ulmighty: this is how I refer to our, Ultimate Creator.

Dimensions, Planes and Realms: are the same thing. In John, 14:2 Christ said, "In my father's house there are many mansions." These mansions are the dimensions. They are planes of reality separated by levels of consciousness. Denser levels of consciousness moving up into higher states of consciousness.

1st Dimension: the mineral kingdom. These are the base substances of consciousness. From these materials other forms can be created.

2nd Dimension: the plant and animal kingdom. Plants, animals, reptiles, etc., have more consciousness than they have been given credit for. This is predominantly due to man projecting his own disconnect from Spirit onto them.

3rd Dimension: the plane of egoic thinking where denser forms of manifestations are seen. This plane houses those Souls who are unaware of their Spiritual Heritage.

4th Dimension: the Astral Plane, also known as, The Emotional Realm. This dimension is the mansion of the Collective Consciousness. It also houses incarnate Beings of a low Light who are either waiting to embody, or who cannot embody because their level of Light cannot reach even the 3rd Plane because of its level of darkness. This is a complex plane, and it is critical to understand it's nature. Which will be further discussed in this book.

5th Dimension: the beginning of the Heavenly Realms. The 5th Dimension has many levels of Heaven within it.

Heavenly Realms: beginning with the 5th Dimension and going all the way up to the Heart of our Creator. The Heavenly Realms are all that is of the Light, including all of the Beings who have ascended into higher states of consciousness. There are many levels within these dimensions, for there are many levels of consciousness. The Heavens are referred to as the Heaven(s) because of the many houses, or dimensions within it.

Frequencies: Frequencies are vibrations. They are the unseen energies of consciousness.

Light: This word is used quite frequently in this book. In these writings Light is capitalized because it is referring to high states of consciousness in the Heavenly Realms. It is a matter of honor and respect. There are certain terms and words that simply do not follow Earthly ways of representation. If I say, Call in the Light, I am saying, call in the highest form of consciousness you are capable of. When I say, Stand in the Light, or Stand in the Truth of the Light, I am saying, stand in the Truth of the highest form of consciousness you can attain, and be firm in your conviction of it. Do not be swayed by levels of egoic thinking. Through this material I will be giving teachings so you may have a more in depth understanding of the Light. I will explain techniques to help you hold and shift the Light.

Truth: capped because it is the reality of the Heavenly Realms. It is consciousness devoid of egoic thinking.

Energetic Bodies, Levels, Fields, Realms: these are interchangeable words meaning the same thing. The basic energetic bodies are the Physical, Emotional and Mental Realms. These bodies can be seen as levels as they lay on top of each other, and they can been seen as fields because they are vast. They are also referred to as Realms because of their individual natures.

Thought Forms: pre-manifested beliefs that are gaining etheric weight in either one's personal consciousness, or the Collective Consciousness.

Spirit: individual or collective Divine connection; either to one's I AM Presence, or the overall identification with the Heavenly Realms.

I AM Presence: the Truth of who we are, our Spirit, our Light, our Consciousness without form.

Co-creator: A being who was created in the image and likeness of our Creator. They have their own I AM Presence, an individual consciousness. Co-creator also means creating in union with others.

Egoic: Ego thinking, man's thinking. Thinking that is based upon the three dimensionality of existence as the supreme reality. Egoic thinking stems from a belief that one is a body, and thus fights for survival of that body. It defends and justifies it's separation from our Creator, and others, because it carries the beliefs of guilt and punishment which it then projects onto the world. Egoic thinking is highly susceptible to the Collective Consciousness, and adds to it readily.

***

*There comes a point when we must decide
if we're going to go all the way
and become who we are.*

CHAPTER I
BODIES OF LIGHT

*We Shine according to the amount of Light we hold.
This Light is our Consciousness.*

LAYERS OF COMMUNICATION

The physical body is a manifestation of the state of consciousness of an individual. That being said, there are Souls who do volunteer to come here bearing an infliction in order to serve. Their consciousness can be in a heightened state in the most significant areas, but they have elected to take on a wound in the physical body which allows them to be in particular areas; teaching the Souls they have elected to serve.

So, the physical body is the manifested vehicle of our current state of consciousness. It's manifestation represents the sum total of who we are in the 3rd Dimension. It is our identifier. It is the way we know Self.

If you picture the layers of an onion and visualize it's core, this will give you an idea of the rings of energetic bodies surrounding the physical body. It is important to understand how these layers interact, as energy is either moving through the fields, or is stuck in a particular field.

These layers are continually communicating back and forth as one receives information, decodes it, sends it back, and receives more information. It is an inward outward movement through the layers. If these layers are clear, our lives will reflect this clarity. If these layers are bogged down, we will experience the ill effects of our beliefs projecting themselves upon the screen of our life.

A negative belief can take form in our mental body; feeling like mental punishment. We can see dramatic scenes played out; tell ourselves we're no good, defend ourselves against accusations, tell other's off; have our very own made for TV movie in our heads. Our goal is to recognize these projections and nip them in the bud before they turn into heavier manifested forms such as depression, or illness. Our work is to figure out why we believe these judgments by searching for the root of the issue and then heal this issue with Truth in the form of facts. Is someone truly out to get us? Are we telling others off because we are afraid our voices won't be heard? If we do not heal these nagging egoic tendencies, they will continue to torment us. They truly are a figment of our imagination. An imagination gone array like a wild horse.

The physical body must be a highly-tuned instrument if we are to hear our Spirit in full force. We simply cannot hear clearly if our bodies are burdened by fear, toxins or are sluggish due to diet. However, there may be times when we have drawn in a large amount of Light and are integrating it into our energy bodies. During this time we may feel lazy, like we have a cold, and may eat more sweets, and the like. This is okay, over time you will learn your own flow. Be patient with yourself during this time. Having high expectations of oneself at any time is not beneficial and blocks our awareness of what is happening.

The physical body is a manifestation of Self. Our consciousness is living in a field of energy which it uses to move about and interact in the 3rd Dimension. Can we handle the idea that we are not our bodies, but Spirit using a body as a vehicle on Earth?

*

The first level surrounding the physical body is the etheric body which is a very fine layer of energy translating the many impressions of the emotional, mental and spiritual bodies to and from the physical body. Like an octave vibrates between the frequencies.

The emotional body is the second layer. It is a sensitive layer. It houses our feelings, moving them through our physical body, and mental body. This layer also picks up information from exterior sources, others as well as the Collective Consciousness. Our emotions are like fuel. They can propel us into behaviors that are positive or negative.

The mental body is more like the stick shift in a car switching gears from the body, through the emotions, through the aura, accessing thoughts from the Collective Consciousness and is capable of absorbing higher levels of consciousness in the Heavenly Realms. It brings this information back through the layers into the physical body, into the brain, and central nervous system.

The chakras are centers of Light running vertically from the base of the spine through the crown center, and beyond. Seven chakras are commonly spoken about at this time. These centers are much more complex than is currently known. For now, the seven chakras are communication centers which can be open or closed according to the level of Light one can handle. Each chakra has their own identifiers, their own functions.

Briefly, the lower three chakras are our Earth based correspondents. They are the root chakra, the sacral chakra and the solar plexus chakra.

The 1st chakra is called the root chakra. It is red in color, and connects us to our life force. If we are connected to Spirit and move this through our body, it is imperative we continue to move this energy into the earth for a solid grounding. If our root chakra is closed off we will experience lethargy and a lack of will.

The sacral, or second chakra is orange in color. It is closely related to our sexual organs, as it is the chakra of creative life force. Sexual, creative energy is powerful and it is helpful to learn how to channel it in a healthy way. When we are feeling incredibly creative, we may also feel sexual. If we want to hone in our creativity, it is important to move the sexual energy up into our Heart Center, or down through our root chakra, and ground it into the earth so we can harness it.

The third, or solar plexus chakra is relationship based, and is yellow in color. We take in energy from others in this area as well as give energy to others from this area. This is why we sometimes here, "This (blank) makes me sick to my stomach". Or, "I get butterflies in my stomach when I see him or her".

The fourth through seventh chakras are related to our connection with Spirit. The heart chakra, throat chakra, third eye, and crown center.

The 4th chakra is our heart chakra, and it is green or pink in color. When this chakra is open, we feel Love, and freely give Love. It is often seen as a lotus flower with pedals opening; as these pedals open, it can feel orgasmic.

The 5th chakra is the throat chakra. Its color is blue and is the seat of our communication. When we are afraid to speak our Truth, we may get a soar throat, or need to clear our throat. Many who have trouble speaking their Truth carry around a turquoise crystal as its energy is linked to communication.

The 6th chakra is the third eye chakra, and is located in the center of the head; the Head Center, when it is open one can access higher states of consciousness. The color of the third eye chakra is indigo.

The crown chakra is the 7th chakra and is purple. The crown chakra is the bridge between Spirit and matter.

When we live in denial, believing in fear; we close down our chakras to one degree or another. We must overcome these fears and beliefs in order to gain Higher States of Spiritual Consciousness. When chakras are in the fullness of their Light they are connected to the vibrations of the Heavenly Realms.

To open the chakras we must raise our vibration. To keep them open we must learn to live in that vibration. Opening the chakras can take some time. As we begin to learn and grow, we begin to trust that it is safe to open our chakras. We begin to realize that we do not depend upon the world outside of us. We do not need the world to bend to our expectations because we know that Spirit does not bend to its expectations. Spirit creates for the highest good for all. There is always a way, a new idea, a new approach. In same, *we* do not need to bend to the world's expectations. We know that we are provided for, will be lead, and have a mission. We do not need approval, we are Angels.

There are many teachings and many ways to open the chakras. Many of them you probably instinctively know but may not be conscious of. They are the things that make you feel good. Whether it is gardening, playing music, painting, cleaning. Whatever makes you happy and joyous is going to raise your vibration. There are techniques such as grounding, exercising, chanting, these are practical and if worked with frequently, will give one the upper edge when the exterior problems of life come to the fore.

Sometimes we get depressed. Things come up in our lives that are unhappy experiences and we get lost and feel alone. In these times we may not have the desire to do what we love. We may be sitting on the sofa like a blob wanting to cry but being unable to let it out. How do we raise our vibration then? Accepting what is happening is the first step. Judging ourselves over being in this state does not help, it pulls us down further. Experiencing the loss of a job, trouble in our family life, a medical issue, these are situations where one can not expect themselves to simply jump from sorrow to joy.

Accepting where we are at is important, it's being good to ourselves. If we need a few hours, or days to move through it, then we need that time and that is all there is to it. When we learn to accept where we are at, we can ask for guidance and we are lead. We may be lead to a friend, a therapist, a teacher or teaching. We may be lead to start walking, or to take a class. Whatever it is we are meant to learn from the situation will come more easily if we surrender to it. Sometimes we have to hand it over to our I AM Presence and the Ascended Host. From the depths of our Heart we say, "I cannot hold this burden anymore, please help me. I let it go into your hands". When we do this, we receive Light because we are letting go of the darkness which binds us.

It is imperative to allow ourselves this process. To stifle it, will only hurt one further. One may be afraid of being judged, or may be told to grow up, or get over it. These accusations are painful and are another's way of hiding from their own feelings, and fears. If you connect to your hurt, then they may have to connect to theirs, and they simply may not be ready. Learning how others project their feelings onto us is important. We need to become ourselves, and we do this by being good to ourselves and honoring what is right for us at the time.

The energy body is an incredible instrument for communication. It is constructed of sacred geometries communicating through Points of Light, and through lines of Light. If you desire to know about the mystery of these, Fields of Light, study the Stars and their formations.

I would like to diverge for a moment and speak about the central nervous system. It is not seen as an energetic body, but it is one of the most critical components of the physical body. The nervous system is affected by the mental and emotional energy picked up from the environment; an exterior experience such as being in a crowded restaurant, or office party. As well as, an internal experience; thoughts and feelings. Our reactions to these experiences send energy through the emotional body and into the brain. The brain decodes it and sends the energy back into the body. Much like an electrical circuit. The more sensitive a person is, the more their nervous system is picking up these energies.

We can understand the workings of this system of energy if we have ever had a feeling of being worried, nervous, agitated, or in the severe form, suffered a panic attack. These types of feelings come from energy moving quickly into and from the brain. We are revved up, and we simply cannot handle the load.

Reigning in the nervous system is an art. To be able to do so, we must become aware of it the moment we feel a rise in this area. If we are in an uncomfortable situation with others, it is best to remove ourselves until we can calm ourselves by taking a few deep breaths, or perform some type of exercise. Breathing regulates the flow of energy and exercising releases energy from our bodies, and is exactly what is needed.

It is important for those around us to respect our need to calm our systems, any further agitation on their part will only make matters worse. We may reconsider relationships with those who trigger our nervous systems on an on-going basis. Being exposed to this type of environment can be destructive, and it inhibits our ability to stay connected to Spirit.

When we are nervous or afraid, the crown chakra, the 7th chakra, is closing. The more the crown chakra closes, the more one is cut off from our Creator. We do not see the crown chakra closing, we feel its effects through the central nervous system. The crown chakra is a threshold between the Heavenly Realms and our consciousness on earth. When open, we experience peace and happiness. When closed, we feel fear, anger and the like.

If one is afraid, they can ask for Light, to be en-lightened on a particular situation. This prayer will be answered in the form of Light. It will move down from the Heavenly Realms and into the crown chakra. It is important to bring it all the way through the body and into the ground. This is a lot of energy. A lot of Light. It has to be anchored. Feeling and consciously guiding the energy through our body and down into the core of the Earth connects us to our environment.

It is a matter of bringing Spirit into the body and being aware of both body and Spirit simultaneously. This is done through physical movement. Physical movement releases memories and imaginations stored in the body. This release helps us become more conscious of ourselves and enables us to take control over our mind and emotions. Focusing on our breathing is another way to ground. When using the breath to ground, it is important to create rhythmic, deep breaths and imagine moving it through our body and into the ground.

The thing to remember about energy is that it is shifted by our consciousness. If all is energy--and it is--then it would stand to reason if one aspect of energy changes, it effects the whole of energy. It can also be affected by the whole.

Once we bite into an apple, the entire energetic structure of the apple is changed. Once we ingest the apple, our energetic structure is changed. The same is true for our world. As we change, the energetic structure of our world changes. Knowing this and focusing our energy here is the trick.

*

The aura is the sum total of all of the interactive layers surrounding the body. It emits the overall energetic mood, or health of a person. It also acts like a filter from exterior energies coming toward oneself.

Another can send a thought toward us, and if we are not the wiser, the energy can attach itself to our aura and effect our thoughts and emotions. If you've ever gone to a shopping mall and for no particular reason started to feel angry, or nervous, it is most likely because you are picking up the energy of the people in the mall. The same is true while driving in heavy traffic areas. Until you are able to hold a more solid construct of Light, I recommend carrying a bit of hematite, or an obsidian crystal to help absorb and deflect some of these energies.

Most of us have heard that saying, "Ugh, they're draining my energy!" If you've ever heard a friend say someone is draining their energy, they are speaking about being around another who attaches a cord to their aura and literally, drains their energy by pulling it from them, siphoning it. Some call these folks, psychic vampires; they feed off of the energy of others. There are many reasons why others do this. For example, they may be passive-aggressive and their way is to be angry at you, not say anything, but pull at your energy. Another is they admire an aspect of you to such a degree, they want it for themselves.

Cord attachment is normal, this is one of the ways we communicate without words. These cords are pure energy. They are like etheric telephone lines, some thicker than others. However, if someone has attached a cord to you and is draining you of energy, or inflicting negative energy toward you, it is advised that this cord be cut and sent back to it's owner. You can do this by visualizing the cord being cut, and both ends being cauterized. Send their portion of cord back to the them and dissolve the cord on your end. You can request Archangel Uriel, or another Angel you work with to help you do this if you need assistance.

We can clear our auras on a regular basis. A practical way is when we shower. Since salt is a transforming mineral, it is often used as a quick way to clear the aura. Take about a quarter cup of sea salt into the shower with you. When you are on your final rinse, simply rub the salt over your body and rinse off. Simple. Try this after a busy day of being out and about, or after attending a gathering that left you feeling in a low mood.

Another way is through meditation. We can picture colors in our auras, and fill them with the color we are drawn to at the time. I do not suggest strong, bold colors. These are powerful and will jolt the system. Soft, diffused colors are the way to go. For example, calling in a delicate pink will give a feeling of tranquility. Calling in white light will clear the aura of debris. Study the meanings of crystals and colors. This will help you understand the energy intensity, the vibrations, of Earth's organic substances, and give you an idea of colors you may want to experiment with.

Sound will clear the aura and give a sense of peace. Drumming is a very effective way to ground, clear energy, and transform energy. Ringing a bell around your chakras, is another quick way to clear.

Archangel Uriel is fantastic with energy work. Call upon Uriel to help you clear and fill your aura with a light that is harmonious to your needs at the time. You may be surprised to be filled with a combination of soft blues, greens, and gold. Perhaps light yellow, white, and gold. There are many combinations that will sooth and heal the energetic bodies, as well as protect them from exterior influences. Be sure to thank Uriel and send him Love.

*

In and of themselves, the mental, emotional, and physical bodies are like clear panes of glass waiting to be impressed upon. Ideally, they would be impressed upon from the Higher Levels of the Divine, and manifest the True expression of one's Spirit.

Since we live beneath the 4th Dimension, we are influenced by it's energy. Our thoughts lift up to it, and so do the billions of thoughts from other people. If we are not aware of this, we will pick up the energy from this realm, as it is all around us. The false ideas carried over time will eat away at the Light we hold within and eventually break down the physical body. Releasing the hold our beliefs have on us restores our Light and our body.

*

Understanding these fields of energy is helpful to us. When we learn to become sensitive to these layers, we can pinpoint where we are stuck and move the energy, which will cause us relief in our physical body, our emotions, and in our thinking.

There are various ways to move energy through our body. One of the best is to simply listen to it. Allow it to speak to us without judging it's messages. Our body knows what it needs because it is connected to the the energetic grids which surround it, the emotions, thoughts, and beliefs we carry. When we listen in this way, strange little things begin to happen. Our body may start to shake or feel warm. If we continue to allow it to, do it's thing, it may bring up memories that it wants to release, false ideas that are believed. The body wants to let go of the burdens that it carries. In and of itself, it is a fantastic machine. It is our consciousness that forces burdens onto the body.

One can also relax, and simply add Light into the cells of the physical body. To do this we visualize the area in our mind's eye. Our mind's eye is sometimes called, the Head Center, the 6th Chakra, the Third Eye. Some teachings say that Christ is speaking about the third eye when he says, in:

Matthew 6:22 (1611 King James Version)
The light of the body is the eye: If therefore thine eye be single, they whole body shalbe full of light.

The light of the body is the eye: Consciousness. Consciousness is Light.

If our eye is single: If we focus our attention upon the Truth that consciousness is pure Light connected to all of Heaven and our Creator; that there is Light, Love and Only Light;

Our whole body will be full of light: This is a natural consequence of holding our consciousness in higher vibrations, which are higher frequencies of Light.

Visualize crystaline light being added into each and every cell of your body. You can sweep this light over areas and direct it into your cells. You will feel the difference as you will be regenerating your cells. I love to use a beautiful green for this. If we hold our mind, our thinking in alignment with our Creator, our consciousness will shine like the sun.

If your energy is not solidified, if you are weak in your fields, beliefs located in your emotional and mental bodies, as well as exterior beliefs from the Collective Consciousness, have an easier time creeping in.

To raise our consciousness to higher levels and maintain clear energetic bodies, we must be willing to surrender what we believe to be true about life. We all have our little ways of justifying what we believe. Our reasons. It is these justifications and reasons that keep us bound to the consciousness of the 3rd and 4th Dimensions. We must be willing to let them go to reach the 5th. In this simple willingness, a bridge is created.

Clearing energies from the 3rd Dimension can be difficult, but not impossible. It depends upon how many false beliefs we carry. Inside of the various images and projections, they become a world unto themselves. We entertain them, feel them, and sometimes even prepare for their arrival. As their power grows, they can manifest. These channels of images and projections are actually the alternate realities that are capable of manifesting. They are alternate because we decide, by the weight of our beliefs, which way our life will take. This is why the Masters have told us repeatedly, Listen to your Heart. This requires strength. We may have a past that is convoluted and hard to discern, this takes time. We have the time. We have all the time we need to heal.

*

Silencing the ego is mastery of Self. The ego exists as long as we have an aspect of believing in our separation from ourselves; our Spirit Selves. This is why we say, climb the Stairway to Heaven. The farther we are from Heaven, a.k.a., the 3rd Dimension of Planet Earth, the lower we are on the staircase. However, much can be learned on this level, and as we walk up the Golden Staircase, we teach what we know to those who are following behind us; just as those in front of us give us the flowering of their experience.

Bringing Light into our bodies and claiming who we are is necessary. We can only get there by silencing the ego. Some teach, let the ego die. This feels negative to me. We tend to associate death with pain and loss. The ego is simply a way of thinking.

Egoic thinking dominates the 3rd Dimension. This is a very old dimension covered with a lot of dust and ashes from previously created lifetimes; the entire history of the planet and those who have lived upon it. We are carrying the weight of our ancestors, if you will. The weight of these beliefs which are housed inside of the Collective Consciousness which lives in the 4th Dimension. The 4th Dimension carries the pre-manifested ideas/emotions of whomever added to it. This is one of the main reasons why Angels are on Earth. We are not necessarily here to save each individual Soul. Although we are lead to such circumstances, our predominant role is to add Light into the 3rd and 4th Dimensions. We do this by understanding what is there and shining our Light upon it. The Ascended Host are sending Light from the Heavenly Realms to assist in this process.

I have heard the term, surrender the ego. This is a tricky word to use. Surrender has various meanings. Some feel surrender as being at the mercy of, or perhaps a giving in. We surrender when we realize we have made an error by believing in the 3-Dimensional Ego. We surrender our beliefs, our fears. To surrender the ego is to let it go.

The basic rule of thumb in conquering the out-of-control manifesting that results from listening to the ego is: Do not let it rule you.

As we saw in the chapter, The Fallen Consciousness, when we began to believe in the exterior world of forms as reality, we created a 3rd Dimensional God who has control of everything, and we suffer the consequences of this God because we believe it is real.

At times we think, I am afraid, and so I will use these pre-defined egoic remedies to rectify the situation. Where is the connection to Spirit in this? Where are the miracles of the Heavens? They are not there. The way up the staircase is this: I am afraid. Connect to Spirit. Connect to the Heavens. Follow the Truth of the matter. There is a Truth. And we strive for the Highest Truth. We know it will be the Highest because we will experience a knowing within ourselves. When we earnestly seek for Truth, we find it. Trusting in the Light of Truth, is our peace, and our power.

It is always up to us to make the connection to Spirit for ourselves, so we may live in our own truth. This truth will always be connected to the One. It takes strength to live in one's Truth, but this strength will be multiplied the more we reach for the 5th Dimensional Truth and begin to live our lives by it instead of a lower level of thinking. We have control. It is only thinking.

God bless the Angels for delivering the Light.

Reaching the 5th Dimension it is simply a matter of letting go of the constructs of the 3rd and 4th Dimensions. Seeing this as pure energy takes the emotional pull out of it and allows us to shift much quicker. When one receives an emotional response based upon a trigger, a memory; even if buried deep inside of the subconscious ego, the moment we feel this, we see it as energy in our mind's eye, and we send Light straight to it. This is a very emotionally detached, and very effective way to make a shift. This can be difficult in the beginning states as it quickly aligns one with their Spirit and this type of shift could feel shocking at first, as one sees the world differently through the twinkling of an eye.

The heaviness of the 3rd Dimension is what makes this shift challenging. If you are having difficulty, feel into the energy and listen to what it is telling you, both in your mind and in your bodies; there will be a correlation. Learn to discern these feelings and understand these messages. Reach out for the Light. The Light assists us in the burning off of this energy. Thus, we become lighter, brighter and trusting in the 5th Dimension instead of being pulled down by the 3rd. The time it takes us to bring in our Light on a continual basis, and then grow that Light, is depended upon the degree in which we are willing to work at it.

Suggestions:

Pray for guidance and wisdom. A book or teaching may come across your path. Feel into it. Is this an ego generated manifestation, or a Spirit lead manifestation? Ask until you are sure. This is learning the difference between the worlds. Every time we question, we are lead to Truth, and then more Truth. Through this we learn how to communicate with our Spirit, and the Heavens, a.k.a., the beauty of creation; a dimension created by conscious Beings whose motive is to reach for the Light of Love. You will learn as you are lead. You will learn what is right for you at the level you are at.

To enter the 5th Dimension is to enter through the Heart energy. The purest point of Light. This purest point of Light lives inside of us because it is our highest consciousness. It is how we are ultimately connected to our Creator. It follows the Light up through the dimensions and into the Heart of our Creator. We get there by calling upon it. What we know as prayer. Communing with our Spirit, the Ascended Host and all of Heaven. It sounds so simple. It is that simple.

Many underestimate the power of prayer because there are so many fancy ways of accessing these realms. It is the Love that we yearn for that calls Heaven. It is our Desire to know this Love, to want to Live in this Love, that brings Heaven to Earth.

Regardless of how far away from the Light we believe we are, we can turn from the ego, touch upon Light, and follow it home. It is a built in mechanism. We cannot be who we are not. We are not at the mercy of creation. We create. Thus we become the master when we master our energy and the energy of the dimensions in which our consciousness resides. Remember, you will live in the belief construct of the dimension in which you place your consciousness. Reaching for the Light is the way to raise one's consciousness. If you were the only person on Earth and there were no teachings whatsoever--you can depend on this method. It is tried and true. The desire of it manifests its fulfillment.

The following chapter will give you more tools to release the ego.

***

YOUR POINT OF LIGHT

Our Point of Light is pure consciousness, our Spirit, our I AM Presence. Being aware of our Point of Light, we begin to make the decisions from this place within us.

We connect to and maintain our conscious connection with our Point of Light by desiring it, by doing those things that help us connect to it, and by surrendering ideas and beliefs that do not have a place within the Light. As we clear our ego, we will strengthen our connection to our Spirit, our Point of Light. From there, we will be lead, in both our spiritual and material lives.

Here is a powerful tool:

Sit in a quiet place where you will not be disturbed for at least a half an hour, the more time one devotes to this, the better.

Take at least three deep breaths. Take each breath in to the lungs in the count of eight, hold it to the count of eight, release it to the count of eight.

When the body is relaxed, you can close your eyes.

The goal is to open the head and crown centers. You may feel intimidated by this. Don't. You are meant to know how to do it.

Picture Light, start at your feet, pulling energy from the earth into yourself and moving it up through the center of your body. As you do this, add Light into your body and into your emotional and mental bodies. As you expand your emotional and mental bodies with light, your chakras become activated. Let them do their thing. Continue focusing on moving the light up the core of your body. You may cough or clear your throat. This is good, it is opening up the throat center, the 5th chakra, and you will know energy is moving. Adjust your body as necessary. You may feel little pockets of energy, bubbles release inside of your physical body. This is also good. If you lose focus, simply reconnect. It is important not to judge yourself or the experience, as this closes down the energy flow and it is only ego projecting it's old fears.

As you pull the energy up through your core, continue on through the middle of your head and out of the top of your head. Feel the energy moving through a vessel of light, a type of energetic tube that can reach far, far into the Heavens. Reach as far as you can. You will know what is comfortable for you, and each time it may change.

Once you are there, expand this vessel, this tube, a little at first and you will be guided as to how far as you advance. Don't push the energy, it will not be effective. Going with the flow is the name of the game.

Do not judge your experience, you may not feel anything happening that is off the charts miraculous. Use the faculties of your imagination. The use of your imagination will link you to the experience. One may say if you do this you are simply imagining it all. That is not true. If something happens in the imagination, we feel it as if it is real. It shifts our energetic centers, and this is what we want to happen.

Inside of yourself say something like, "I call for the Light of the Heavens to clear my ego and release me from it's bondage. I ask for only what I can handle. Bless you and thank you".

Once you feel the connection has been made and it is time to come back, draw the Light of the Heavens into your vessel and gently close it to it's original tube like structure. See the energy moving back through the top of your head, and down the core of your body. Picture the energy moving through your physical, emotional and mental bodies.

At this point what you want to do is reinforce the outer boundaries of your aura. You can picture a golden white light around the edges of your aura. Trust that it is there. The golden white light is a wonderful form of protection.

Overtime you will become adept at this. Reaching up to the Heavens will be second nature. You will be able to do this in any circumstance, eyes open, standing in the grocery store line. As your mental and emotional bodies carry more Light, it will be a quick elevator ride into Heaven and a quick elevator ride back down to Earth.

*

There are also prayers that are very powerful. Speaking these will invoke energies from the Ascended Masters. I've included some of these in the chapter, Angelic Prayers. A word of caution, go slow. When we invoke light to clear the ego, the ego shows itself and if we are not accustomed to recognizing it, it can throw us.

Example: I've said the prayers, done the meditation, and I'm moving through my daily life. A strong emotional situation arises. Someone has said or done something that really pushes my buttons. I react. There is turmoil. One might think, "Hey, I called in the Light and I get this!?" The answer is, yes. It is the ego being revealed by the Light. This has to happen in order for us to recognize it and put it in it's place.

Don't worry, not every ego belief will come up at once. Although some of them may be a bit dramatic in the beginning, they get easier as time rolls on because we are learning to master them. Here is a thought that may waylay your fears and encourage you to continue in this work, the ego is going to continue to manifest if you are unconscious of it; better to clear it and get on with your life. Invoking the Light will clear the ego so one is not at its mercy time and again.

When one of these egoic situations rises, notice your reaction to it. Ask yourself if this reaction is based on Truth or an exterior stimulus. If it is based on an exterior stimulus, an ego belief, and you sincerely want to clear it, you will have a revelation and be able to shift your thinking.

The revelation will be the Truth that you can use to stand up to ego.

You will be able to say, "No! I know that Spirit is creator of all things and I do not have to believe that this financial situation is going to ruin my life. No! I do not have to stay in this job, relationship, etc. because Spirit can move me to a situation that is better suited for me". It is simply putting the matter in the hands of our Spirit self, not in the hands of false beliefs that are based on past limited agendas.

Our Spirit is not intimidated by life; the ego is intimidated by life.

Over time our relationship with our Spirit self, our I AM Presence, will become a natural part of our lives. The Truth of the matter will come upon us quickly, and we will use this information to silence the ego.

Remember, the ego is merely a voice in our head.

***

CHAPTER II
LIVING BETWEEN THE WORLDS

In effect, Here is Everywhere.

INTRODUCTION

The ability to Live between the Worlds comes through understanding what these worlds are. There are many worlds. In this case, we will focus on the reality that we have been taught, and the Spiritual Reality that is the Ultimate Reality.

When we begin to understand manifestation and get a real sense of how our beliefs create our personal world, there is a period of adjustment. "Wait a minute, what I've been taught doesn't ring true to this!" We get miffed because our entire ego has been blown; our entire sense of security in the world is threatened, and we often do not know how to pick up the pieces as manifestation can move rather quickly being layered with our many beliefs.

One by one, we begin to work with shifting these beliefs. As we do this, we see the magic of how the universe works, and most importantly, cares for us.

Moving back and forth through different stages of consciousness is, Living Between the Worlds. The consciousness of having little money to pay a bill, and trusting it will be paid. One world is the bill. One world is the belief in the Truth of Spiritual fulfillment; we create our reality. We can draw money to us.

Living Between the Worlds is understanding there is a Higher Truth; the Freedom of Spirit is not controlled by ego. Ego can only limit Spirit if we allow it to. Living in ego is living in one world. Living in Spirit is living in another. We live in our Higher Truth while simultaneously experiencing the effects of our manifestations; and the manifestations of others. We learn from our manifestations and move into even higher states of consciousness.

Two states of consciousness. One always egoic thinking. One always Spiritual thinking. Riding between these two worlds is also called, the Middle Way. Knowing how the Spiritual Realm works, and bringing it down to Earth. By learning the many distinctions between these worlds, an Angel is able to glide through them.

It is time to let go of the world you know and take hold of who you are. Angels are supernatural Beings. We are not at the mercy of the 3rd Dimension. If we can get this, truly get this, we can shift the 3rd Dimension radically. This is bringing consciousness to Earth. Our Presence hails the 5th Dimension because we are made of Light, created to do this very thing. We are a magnet to supernatural energy. I must make a disclaimer for those who want to, 'test their supernatural abilities'. Do not start yourself on fire, jump off a cliff, or do some random act of stupidity to try to prove this to yourself. When the time comes for you to be at this level of consciousness there will be nothing to prove.

Spirit does not move the way man moves. Spirit has it's own way. Spirit sees all of the possibilities. We can get an intuitive nudge telling us to bring our car in, TODAY. We don't know why. Our ego mind panics. "I have to take Jimmy to the volley ball game. My wife needs to go to her sisters!" When we learn to listen and we bring the car in, we find out later we had a loose motor mount and if we didn't bring it in, we could have been stuck on the freeway, if we were lucky, because our motor could have fallen straight to the ground while we were driving.

Spirit sees. Spirit knows what we do not know in our limited egoic thinking. Learning to let go of expectations and attachments will bring us further up the Golden Ladder, and once we are up there, our understanding will deepen and will help us navigate between the worlds.

Once we understand these worlds, and trust in what we have learned in Spirit, the easier our life will be. We will not be stressed or taken over by problems. We know there is an answer, and we know the answer will come. Trust and Letting Go are two main Keys used in Living Between the Worlds.

Learning ways to stop the panic of egoic thinking and keeping ourselves in higher states of consciousness for longer periods will help fortify our newfound life.

The tools in the following chapters will help you navigate between the worlds, the Middle Way.

***

SPIRITUAL DISCERNMENT

Angels naturally have the Gift of Spiritual Discernment, something we need in order to follow Spirit in any situation. This gift is greatly enhanced by our growing sensitivity to energy and Spiritual Truth.

What is Spiritual Discernment?

Spiritual Discernment is being able to see past the illusion or facade of a person or situation. Spiritual Discernment is being able to identify egoic thinking, egoic beliefs and behaviors. Being able to judge Truth from untruth.

Spiritual Discernment does not use logic to judge people or situations. Spiritual Discernment is being receptive to energy and being able to read that energy. We hear and feel into the sound of a voice. We experience vibration and interpret it by the emotional reaction we receive.

We know our discernment is working well when we are tuned-in to our Energetic Bodies. When we know how to read our own bodies, we are in a better position to know what is coming into them. We feel into the emotions being felt. We feel into the scene. What energies are here? I am picking something up, what is it? Sometimes we don't know. There is a sense but we can't put our finger on it. This is okay, we may be picking something up that is there, but we are not meant to do anything about it. We also might be picking up our own fears. When we are not connected to our body, relaxed in who we are, our chakras close; this constricts the Light flowing into us. Breathing deeply opens up our awareness and raises consciousness.

Focusing on the breath as a way to calm and center the body can be done easily. It's just a matter of focusing on your breathing, and feeling into patterns of breath that work for you. Deep, slow, out of the mouth; out of the nose. Moving the air into our lungs, or diaphragm. Experiment with depth of breath and the timing of it. Do not try to force yourself to do traditional breathing techniques. If they do not work for you this could become a judgment against Self as not living up to the, 'way'. We must get used to controlling our own physical bodies by listening to them. After all, they are ours, and they have their messages.

Feeling into the patterns of breath, we learn to regulate our awareness. Breath brings Life into the body by centering, and balancing our nervous system. It allows us to relax, which allows the chakras to release their protective hold against fear. If we are listening to our bodies, they will give us the awareness that comes with that type of release. Also, we will gain Light. We can move this Light throughout our cells and regenerate.

Awareness is Light. Light is Consciousness. Pure Consciousness. Which is why our Creator is an Incredible Sun. So, let go, and enter the flow.

*

One time I was walking through a busy city. A man was standing curbside, yelling and swearing. I knew right away he had a demon. He was being possessed. My heart went out to him. I prayed for him, and asked what I could do. I was told, sometimes it is not for you to do anything. As I began to walk by him, he instantly quieted and stayed quieted. I knew that he knew who I was. At the time, I felt horrible for only being able to walk by. Then it came to me, I did do something for him. The Light of my Presence gave him the opportunity to have Light. The Light of my Presence gave him the chance to touch Light, and to experience it. This was a Mission. An Angelic Mission. One where I gave and also learned.

Now I know my Presence; the Light of my consciousness, has a profound effect on others and the environment, and the reality of my being an Angel became clearer to me.

Of course those who were walking by him were radiating some form of Light. Some negative; some positive. But not enough Spiritual

Light to have this effect. The spirit who possessed this man had no choice but to bow to the Light. Because of this, it gave the man an opportunity to feel his own Spirit, and make the connection stronger to it.

Amazing how these things can happen in the middle of a busy city. No one being the wiser except him and I.

*

Spiritual Discernment comes, first and foremost, with a Desire to Love. When we Love, our Heart opens and we see, feel, and hear, what is going on in the world around us; in the deeper sense. From this sense we will know whether we are to add Light, dissolve Light, heal, or speak.

We do not need to be afraid if we are doing the right thing or not. As soon as we worry about this, our chakras close, and our ability to discern is lessened. Keeping the chakras open, being relaxed and trusting, is the best way for us to be able to use our discernment wisely. Over time we will be able to trust what we are picking up, and trust that we will be moved according to how Spirit wants to move us.

We must always look for the deeper Truth of a person or situation to see beneath the facade, the masks of projection by self and others. One may present angry, when really, they are hurting inside, cut off from Spirit, unable to see. Another may be behaving in a very detached way, self-absorbed and careless. Any ego projection is going to be void of Light. It is our job to look under the ego projection and attend to the Co-creator's Soul, which has been temporarily separated from their connection to their own I AM Presence and our Creator. From this place we can do the highest work, for this is the Highest Truth.

It is advised not to push one's Light toward another who does not want it. In same, it is advised to not allow another to push darkness toward you. It is important to claim our Light. To claim the Truth of ourselves. We are Angels and that is just a simple fact. Living this out in the world takes time, people are not used to it. At times we may pull back our Light in order to make others feel comfortable. At times this is advised, at other times it cheats them out of having to see themselves and therefore make a change. We will know how to balance this over time as our sensitivity to the use of Light and Wisdom grows.

*

Alice Bailey talks about the Glamours. A Glamour feels like looking at a projection screen. You are seeing images. They are images which are played out on the stage of life, as we know it. Some of these Glamours are powerful. One such Glamour would be the obsession with the physical body. This is not, "Glamour" as in fashion. Glamour is projected illusion onto the world of form.

When I feel a Glamour, I feel it outside of my body. I am looking at it from a distance. I can feel the energy as if I am looking through a gigantic aquarium. I am separated from it by a force field. Much like watching a play. One can get drawn into it, or watch it from the sidelines.

Once you get used to sensing Glamours, you'll be surprised how many of them you see. It is very much like walking through a play, but not being one of the actors. The actors believe the play. You do not.

As Angels, we can use our Light to dissolve some of the fog off of these Glamours, simply by being aware of them. This awareness creates Light and new perceptions in the Collective Consciousness.

*

It's not always easy being an Angel on Earth. We see what others don't see. We see what they don't want us to see. And sometimes they can't handle it. We know we are not judging them, but they do not always feel that way. Patience. When I feel lonely, I reach out to Spirit. I lay under the stars and receive their Loving Light.

Our Spiritual Discernment grows when we raise our vibration and are connected to our own I AM Presence. Our discernment grows when we come from a True Desire of wanting to Love others and Live in Love. With this desire, much knowledge is given to us and our bodies begin to hold more Light. The Light that we carry is really the conductor of our ability to sense the world around us.

As we begin to let go of ego judgments and expectations, and yearn to live in the Truth of Spirit, Light pours down into us according to what we can handle. As we begin to understand the Light within us, learn to use it, and move according to our intuition, our Spiritual Discernment will flourish.

***

MIGHTY MESSENGERS

For an Angel, the receiving and giving of messages is one of our highest callings. We are specialists in our fields and in this particular field we go through a lengthy training process. We must come to know the arena in which we serve. We must clear ourselves, our intentions, and step down information through the dimensions, and translate that information in a cohesive, succinct fashion.

Our ability to speak Truth depends upon our ability to hold a field of dimensional energy long enough to communicate what we receive.

It is imperative that one be transparent, with little to ideally no ego, in order to give messages. We must be adamant about stepping away from our own fears or desires. The messages are about, and for, those whom we serve. This takes practice on Earth because there are so many distractions. We also need to discern the consciousness of the person the message is for, and the effects the Astral Plane has on him or her. Once we know how they are influenced, we can translate the message in such a way as to slip it past their ego. However, there are times where we must be direct and cannot be concerned about anyone's ego.

Angels are able to move their consciousness into points on the grid, to a specific place, or to many. Because we are all connected, we form a type of energetic grid. We do not see this grid with our human eyes, but it is there. If you look up at the stars, you will eventually see lines of light between them. This is an example of an energetic grid. It is important to understand; this grid is not a fixed grid. It shifts as our consciousness shifts. Each Soul is a Point of Light within this grid. It is how we communicate without words. This is what some on Earth call, Telepathy. It is the exchange of Light between us.

Light sends messages, energy, which can either heal or weaken another depending upon it's vibration. Transmitting negative messages is a low level of vibration. I have seen it as a frantic, sometimes sparky red. Other times I have seen it as grey, with a slow moving tone. Positive energy is vibrant and life giving. This of course, is the most optimum. This is what the Heavenly Realms are made of, and why they are so beautiful and crystalline in nature.

Angels have a strong telepathic component because of our ability to hold Light. According to our level of Light, we can contact anyone, anywhere and send Light. We can envelop another in a blanket of Light should they be in sorrow or unable to do so for themselves. Angels can also send protective energy, and call upon other Angels for help in all areas. We can move fast through the grid.

The reason some can see Angels at certain times, generally in times of great need, is because they are in a state of consciousness, which is open; they are crying out.

Some of these times are when there are accidents, and the like. In this type of situation, one is usually in a state of shock, they often dissociate from their everyday thought processes. In this dissociated state, an aspect of themselves is more connected to the Spiritual Realms. They are more receptive, and thus they can see beyond physical reality. Beyond the 3rd Dimension. The Heavenly Realms are communicating to these Souls in a way they can comprehend.

There are also those times of great change, when the Souls of the Earth are about to experience a shift in consciousness, such as the birth of Christ. In these cases, Angels are seen because the Truth of their message depends upon them being seen. It gives the Heavenly Realms the credibility that is sometimes needed to get the message through to 3rd and 4th Dimensionally covered Souls.

In the Heavens, thought transference is normal communication. The Ascended Host transmits energetic codes, and frequencies through the dimensions. Sound and Light are extremely fast, so it doesn't take long, in fact in most cases it's instantaneous. Angels on Earth are able to hear the messages coming through very clearly if we are able to keep ourselves in a calm and open state. Panic, depression, or any vibrationally low mood will close down the communication channels and make it difficult or impossible to hear. Yet, even in these times when I've called for help, although muddled, I did get direction. This is what has helped me learn the importance of holding myself in a receptive energetic state.

Telepathy is used in distance healing. One can speak to another across the miles and sense energetically what is occurring within them and their life. We can send energy to them focusing on the areas that need assistance. We do not have to speak with them over the phone because we can contact them through these channels of Light. Angels are gifted in this way for obvious reasons. We are messengers, healers, and we often need to be in several places at once. The proof that is available in this regard, is the result. I am sure if you are an Awakening Angel this has been a fun adventure and a curious one. Knowing that you can instinctively sense energy across the miles and work with it gives one confidence in their abilities and the desire to grow. In giving Light, one gains Light and is given more avenues to serve.

How does one enhance their Telepathic Abilities?

What is required is becoming sensitive to energy itself. There are many roads to this, Chi-Gong, Reiki, Energy Healing, the Light Body, Dancing or Playing Music. If one studies under a teacher or reads about energy, I encourage teachings that come from the Ascended Host, written by a trusted source; which you will know by its resonance. They are often in-line with, and are extensions of other teachings that you know are true. Extension does not necessarily mean the same teacher. Your Spiritual Discernment will guide you to what is right for you. Trust it.

Although Science is becoming more interested in this area, they are coming from an after-the-fact point of view. Science studies manifestation after it's manifested, which can only take them to a certain point of discovery. Knowing and discovery are two different things. When one is in a heightened state of awareness, they know. It does not matter how they know, this is immaterial to what they know; the knowledge itself is what is useful.

One can only gain Spiritual Knowledge by lifting their vibration. One can only lift their vibration by proving themselves by predominantly mastering the vibration they are in, with an intension to move forward in the Light of Love. If one were to raise their vibration and then try to use knowledge gained from that state for selfish ego manifestations, they will reap what they sow at the lower level of vibration of selfishness and ego. Of course, this is not encouraged.

Personally, I have found my training in the Light Body techniques extremely powerful. Prior to learning these techniques, I would get sensations and pulls in my energetic bodies, but didn't really understand what was happening, nor that I even had energetic bodies. This went on for a long time. I had asked those around me, even those who were healers in the church, but they did not know themselves. When I realized this was not the norm, I asked our Creator for help.

Soon after, I was lead to a book written by Sanaya Roman, The Power of Personal Awareness. This book confirmed so many things for me regarding personal boundaries and energy. At the back of the book was information about the Light Body. I called straight away and was connected to a teacher. Over the phone the teacher was able to help me understand the sensations I was experiencing. I was invited to a class. After going on one of the meditation journeys, I just instinctively knew this was the next step for me. It was a very exciting time. I felt like I was coming home.

The Light Body that I have studied, has it's own set of frequencies which move through and outside of the physical body. Toning, sounding the notes of these frequencies causes us to become aware of them and use them in various ways; raising our consciousness, transmuting negative issues in our lives, drawing abundance, and speaking with Ascended Masters and our Planetary Logos.

Through these teachings, I became increasingly sensitive to energy, and was able to move through the lessons at lightening speed, even at the curiosity of my teacher. Time went on and I began to explain other sensations to her, sensations that were not taught in the Light Body techniques. In those, she could not guide me. From then on, I had no choice but to receive my teachings from the Ascended Host who spoke to me and led me to various teachings, and situations.

Energy Healing was another avenue for me. I was able to learn more about how the body holds energetic patterns. What I love about this field of study is it just plunges right into working with energy itself. It's a sort of, cut to the chase, philosophy. Although, it is imperative not to rush healing this way. When we shift energy in a person's body, their consciousness shifts. If they are unprepared for this shift, it could make matters worse for them.

In later years, Spirit lead me to move to a very quiet location. In this location I was able to sense and hear without the noise pollution of typical city life. Without knowing how it came, I began to distance heal friends and family. I could contact them through Spirit and touch in; sensing what was going on in their life. I could send Light to them at distances and comfort them.

That being said, it is not necessary to move to a quiet location. Prior to my living in one, I was growing anyway. At that time, I was meant to be around people to pick up their energy and learn how to shift it from that playing field. One can simply drive to nature to recharge when need be. One can meditate or imagine themselves in nature as well. The imagination, the ability to put oneself in another energetic field is just as real as being there, because it is an energetic field. If one is meant to move to a quiet location, one will be lead. One of the things I often remind myself of is the reality that I am on a mission. This helps me when I am tempted with ego desires.

*

I can only give you an overall instruction as to how to receive and give messages because there are too many situations and too many levels of consciousness to get into these types of details. You may be living in Kenya where the communication style, the history of myths, or religions, are different than where I live. Everything you need to know about receiving and sending messages comes from the amount of Light you hold; the information you receive is an inherent aspect of that Light. This is why I've been using the word Light so much throughout this book. It really is about Light. The amount of

Light you hold is the amount of consciousness you carry. Once your consciousness is raised, all of the instructions you need are within that consciousness. The Ascended Host and other Angels are always happy to assist us in raising our consciousness; all we need to do is simply ask.

When Heaven sends a message through us to an individual, it is because this Soul is requesting some form of help. We may be having a casual conversation, then something pops through our mind, we say it, and voila, it is the message. The Soul whom it is meant for has a moment of revelation, and is generally surprised and delighted. Often they say, "Isn't that funny? I was just thinking about that. What a coincidence".

Sometimes we will be directed to a person to give a hand in this or that. Being directed, and moving forward in our own idea of service, are not the same thing. It is not advised to move forward on one's own accord. Of course helping others is what we do, but if the Heavens are telling you, no. Then it is, No. We do not need to know why. Many times I want to know why. Then I realize that what is truly important is that I trust there is a reason and I must stay true to my course. This is trust. I must trust for my own life, and for the life of others. Heaven knows better than I when to intervene.

*

The Basics: Sensing. Clearing. Asking for Wisdom. Translating. Transmitting.

When Asked for Guidance by a Co-creator:

Feel into the situation and be clear on your read of it. Ask yourself questions. You want to make sure you are not coming from *your* perspective, but the perspective of the person whom the message is for. Someone might ask, "Aren't Angels supposed to already know?" Often we do. Sometimes, the coloring of the 4th Dimensional Astral Realm can get a little cloudy. After all, we are living on Earth under the rather dense forms of the Collective Consciousness, and some of us are more evolved than others. Praying for Wisdom is always advised.

Ask for direction, and be receptive to that direction. If we are open, and willing, the 5th Dimension will send back the information and guidance needed. It is our job to make sure we are clear, and our intentions are coming from Love. In this way, the information will come straight through the Astral Plane without hindrance.

We must interpret the transmission, a.k.a., answer to prayer, in the language of the Soul it is intended for. This does not mean literal foreign languages, unless we are called to that arena. In the beginning we will start in the area in which we live and have our being. We have all grown up in specific areas. We know the dialect of the people we live around, the slang, the vibe of the day. We know how our towns, cities, states, and with the internet, the world at large, communicate. We each have our area of coverage, so we are meant to be who we are in order to reach those we are meant to reach.

Our goal is to give the message in a way the recipient is able to hear. We ask the Ascended Host to prepare the recipients heart for this message. We can feel the energetic level of this Soul. In that, we know how much Light they are able to carry. We realize where we need to be careful in speaking. Do we need to keep it short and sweet? Do we need to be direct? It may help to put one's hand on their Heart. This will help you center, connect you to your intension, and to Spirit. Over time, you will find what works best for you. Be comfortable in that. There is nothing worse than feeling we must conform to doing things in specific ways. Spirit flows, and it's energy connects to us in the way that is unique to our own vibration.

This may sound like a complex list of things to do, particularly when one finds themselves in a pinch. In many ways, this comes as second nature to you. The more you realize who you are, an Angel, it will become just a matter of fact.

If Heaven is Sending You on a Mission:

Sometimes, Heaven has a message of its own, and when Heaven is sending you, you will know it. You will be primed for the job. One day, you are directed this way and that, finding yourself in front of a total stranger. It doesn't matter who this person is, beggar, businessman, preacher, or store clerk. Maybe a town meeting, or a board meeting. Sometimes, larger arenas. If you are capable for the mission, you will be sent. Perhaps, you are the only one who can be sent; with ease. Of course, Heaven waits for no one, and there is always an Angel to serve. However, we will not feel ourselves if we grow lazy and dismiss our gifts. Our lives will become dull and we will grow increasingly unhappy.

In the beginning, it might feel awkward, one may feel a little unsure of themselves. It's okay. Practice. Practice by asking for help, and getting into the teachings that present themselves to you. They come to you for a reason. Study them, and study them well. Question them, and question them well. A teaching may come across your path much like the Fallen Angel book came across mine.

I was not directed to that book because I was meant to believe in what it said. In fact, it was just the opposite. I was meant to know of it's existence and it's teaching, in order to shift the Collective Consciousness to the Truth, and then bring this Truth to others; this is an example of Heaven sending a message of it's own.

Transmuting Energy:

There will be times when we are called into a bigger arena to speak Truth. People may come against you, you may feel intimidated. This is the perfect time to Transmute the energy.

Ground yourself by dancing, walking, or doing some physical activity where you move your body, connect to the Earth and to your physical body. While you do this you will feel both the intensity of the problem and the energy of your body.

Call the Light. Feel the Light moving into your Crown Center at the top of your head and down through all of your chakras.

Pull the energy back up from the Earth and into your 6th chakra. You may see and/or feel the intensity of this movement of energy. Move the Light you have gathered into it. Your goal is to dissipate the situation with Light. Bath it in Light, Dissolve it in Light.

Whatever way works naturally for you. Continue to add Light to this situation until you feel it shift. Then stop and Bless the situation. You may feel the need to do this several times, each time, stop when your Spirit tells you to, you will know when this is. Respect Spirit's wishes and do not push Light when you are asked to stop sending Light. Rest, take it easy, you will be amazed at the results. And Bless the results. It is always good for us to remember; those around us may be unconscious. When we bless them, we give them the opportunity to come to the Light.

*

Of course, some will read this and say, you don't have to be an Angel to do these things. Well, you can certainly use the practical tips if you are not an Angel, and this is encouraged. The more Souls that tap into the 5th Dimension, the more Light can come to Earth. The difference being, Angels are created to do this.

Angels are on Earth to specifically bring in the Light so that Co-creators can learn to do these things on their own. We Anchor the Light and send Heavenly Realms of Light into and through the 4th Dimension specifically for this purpose. Once the Co-creators on Earth have risen their consciousness to a certain level, some Angels will stay, and some will elect to go to another dimension. We may even be called to another dimension. We never run out of things to do because our Creator is forever expanding, thus, the dimensions are always expanding. We are the Agents of Expansion.

It is of critical importance that our motive is always as pure as possible. Sometimes this is difficult as we may be emotionally pulled this way or that. Work through it. Heaven wants a clear connection and will send aid. Our job is to reach up for this connection from our Hearts.

Of course, there will be times when we flub up. When our emotions get the best of us, our fear, our anxiety. We might snap and then eat a bag of potato chips in a rush of overwhelm. Don't beat yourself up. You're living on Planet Earth. This is a tough playing field. Just keep bringing yourself back into the Light. What generally happens when we dip in consciousness is we have a renewing of compassion for the Co-creators living under the cloud, and more compassion for ourselves.

Receiving and sending messages are forms of art, and they take practice. Once we become sensitive in this area, our ability grows.

Remember, Heaven is on our side. We are Angels, High Bright Points of Light streaming down from the Heavenly Realms. Created to serve. Created to give Life. This is one of our finest gifts and we are meant to use it. We will be given all the assistance we need, and more.

***

INVOKING THE LIGHT

Invoking the Light is not the same as calling in our Angelic I AM Presence. Although we must do this in order to, Invoke the Light, we Invoke the Light in order to command it. As an Angel, this is a part of our job.

My knowledge and experience in Commanding the Light came to me when I became aware of the magnitude of the pull in the Collective Consciousness. In this teaching, Invoking the Light, means to call it in for the express purpose of dissolving beliefs inside of the Collective Consciousness. This is service on a much larger scale than clearing one's individual energetic bodies.

These are areas where the Co-creators are blind to themselves; what they believe, and what they are creating. This call originates from the Co-creators themselves, as their Hearts of pain reach up into the Heavenly Realms, and the Heavenly Realms respond. The Ascended Host respond by sending Light from the Heavens, and the Angels work from inside of the dimension itself.

You will be called to Invoke the Light. We do not take control of the situation ourselves. We will be moved and we will answer. We were created to answer. It is in our nature. We live to, Command the Light because we are Light Bearers. Light Bearers Protect the Light. Expand the Light. We use the Light in any dimension we are called to use it. We can harness it at many levels and send it accordingly.

One who is of third dimensional thinking, one who is locked into ego forms, or who desires to try to use this commanding of the Light for their own purposes will not be able to. This Truth, the ability to use this technique is only given to those who are responsible in their use of it.

Those who pervert these teachings cannot rise up into higher dimensions, for we all reap what we sow when we sow. This is not a punishment. This is a reality. This is a natural consequence of manifestation and nothing more. To go around making statements regarding the reaping of karma in a tone of condemnation is not of the Heavenly Realms. It is an accusation based upon raising oneself above another. What we judge from ego, the Heavenly Realms see as unconsciousness. They are very aware of the pain that comes due to unconsciousness, this is why they send in Light, and of course, why the Angels are here.

There is also another call. This is the call coming directly from the Ascended Host. This call has to do with boundaries. For as much as Co-creators have the right to create, even unconsciously, they do not have the right to override the Free Will of others. This particular aspect of the Collective Consciousness has take time to shift because many of the Souls living under oppression are unconscious of it themselves, and they actually add to the dilemma by not doing anything one way or another. This creates stagnation inside of the lower dimensions. Stagnation is not a part of the overall plan and because of this, it is not allowed to last for long, even though it may seem long upon the Earth Plane. Yet, if you look around you, you will see there have been many changes since the 1950's. Some of them good, some of them not so good. Spiritual Evolution is occurring in this way so that Co-creators can learn who they are. The Heavenly Realms are not going to interfere at every juncture because that defeats the purpose. Co-creators need to learn who they are, and how to use their own abilities.

*

Angels, we will always be called to serve at the level of our expertise, in this case, the thought forms we can handle. We will be shown the belief systems that hold sway inside of the Collective Consciousness. We will feel the various fears which emanate from these beliefs. Through our emotional connection to this we are ready to work.

We call in the Light of Truth either by the use our vocal facilities, or by the use of the power of our mind. It is all about intension. Some of us will speak in different languages. In some religions this is referred to as speaking in tongues. Angels are adept at moving through the dimensions and know the language, and sounds, of these dimensions. These sounds are vibrations which are able to move into and through various frequencies. Some sounds are more powerful than others. Our knowledge of this happens as a matter of fact, it is not something that we must go and study. Although, learning about tones, mantras and such will help us open in this area. The languages that move through us are spontaneous, and over time will be able to connect to the full consciousness of their vibration. Practice and Trust. Trust and Practice.

By the time you get to this level of service, you will know how to connect. Sometimes this is a wrestle. As we reach up for the Light from the 5th Dimension, the 4th Dimension pulls upon us. We must stand in the Light. We must not believe one single word of ego that emanates from the Collective Consciousness. We must not buy into it whatsoever. As I tried to demonstrate in my conversation with the darkness inside of the Collective Consciousness, one can see the many slippery ways in which the voices of the 4th Dimension try to cling to us. It is as if emerging from muddy waters.

We are called to this when we will feel the weight of the Souls on Earth adding fears into the Collective Consciousness. When we feel this weight, we pray to the Heavens for wisdom. We counsel with the Ascended Masters, and transmute the energy.

Wanting the Light, calling in the Light, is Invoking the Light.

Heavenly Father, preserve the purity of our Light. May we desire it above all else, and bring Heaven to Earth. Amen.

***

STEPPING DOWN THE LIGHT

If you are able to rise up into the 5th Dimension, it is imperative to try, as best you can, to not allow your thoughts to become distorted by the 4th Dimension on their way back down. Doing so will cloud, so to speak, your ability to command the Light.

Stepping down the Light is moving the Light down from the 5th Dimension and higher into the lower dimensions. We do this in the same way we reach up. We do not take no for an answer. We do not bend to the whims of the 4th Dimension, or the pleas of the discarnate Souls who live there. We are bringing down the Light and that is all there is to it.

Negotiations do take place. There are times when the Heavenly Realms are questioned whether or not the Light will be too much or should be directed in this way or that. These negotiations are generally brought up by the Beings in the 4th Dimension. Learning to spot their cunning ways is important. The negotiations happen through the use of measuring Truth against what is being proposed. These negotiations take place much like a senate meeting, or a courtroom. Those who request the negotiations are generally asking for more time. The negotiations themselves are, at times, nothing more than a stall tactic. The thought forms, the consciousness of these forms simply do not want to be disintegrated. The Beings who are connected to these thought forms, who empower them with their beliefs, are not wanting to change. Much of it is out of ignorance. Some Beings simply do not understand that their hanging onto these outdated beliefs is hurting others, and themselves, unnecessarily.

I have been at high counsel meetings in the Heavenly Realms where there is much at stake. Some Souls on Earth are not reaching up for the Light, other Souls are using their manifesting skills through egoic thinking, and these Souls and the planet itself suffer because of it. The Ascended Host wants to send Light, and there are many questions and objections to move through. A decision is reached, and Light rushes forth the moment it is commanded.

Angels, we have a responsibility to bring Light to Earth. We do this by Invoking the Light, and by our determination to bring it down into the 3rd Dimension.

***

ANCHORING THE LIGHT

Angels are Beings of Light created with the purpose of holding the Light wherever they are sent. Being born in a physical body on Earth, Angels have the ability to hold, anchor, the Light early on. Depending upon our upbringing both in our chosen families, race, cultural orientation, and country, we can be influenced and taught to hide our Light, which is our Divine Expression. Eventually, the Angel in us will come out, and to the degree we can accept this is to the degree we can shine.

The more powerful Angels, like the Archangels, hold extreme amounts of Light. If this magnitude of Light were simply allowed to flow in its fullness upon the Earth, the consciousness of the Beings living here could not handle it. The Light would simply burn up their consciousness and destroy their sense of individuality.

As it stands now, many people are being affected by the Light that has already been sent in. The Light reveals the darkness, so Co-creators are having to deal with the many false beliefs they carry, not always an easy thing to do for those who do not want to let go.

The Heavenly Realms give us Grace during this time. They realize some of us are afraid to let go because we have not learned what will be there for us when we do let go. Some are heavily ego-invested to the point of being terrified. Some are afraid they will be greatly punished for what they have done. They will not be punished, they will simply go to the dimension of their state of consciousness. Now is the time that there is Grace. Now is the time for all Beings to turn to the Light. For, there will be a time when the amount of Light that is anchored upon the 3rd Dimension will force darker aspects of consciousness into other dimensions. Those who hold a higher state of consciousness will rise to the 5th Dimension, and those who do not will find themselves either back in a new 3rd Dimension, or as a discarnate being in the 4th Dimension, the Astral Realm. There are many steps in each dimension, each moving higher as one's consciousness is raised.

We Anchor the Light by claiming it. We Anchor the Light by claiming who we are. We stand in the Truth of who we are. When we stand in our Truth, Light comes to us and through us, surrounding us. We expand our Light by feeding it Truth. By claiming more and more of the Truth of who we are and the Truth that abides in the Heavenly Realms. We hold to our Truth. We defend the boundaries of our Truth by fighting off ego projections and putting them in their place. This strengthens our Light and from here we will be given more.

***

WIELDER OF THE LIGHT

Once we have called in the Light, brought it back down and harnessed it, we are ready to direct it.

We direct it as we are instructed. We will know we are being instructed because we will be given the coordinates: This is where to direct the Light, here is the thought form inside of the Collective Consciousness that needs to be dissolved.

Something happens when we dissolve thought forms in this way. We will begin to see the world around us change. There are suddenly new insights, new ideas are brought to the fore, and we may be stunned at how quickly this happens. What we worked on six months ago is coming to fruition. We see it and exclaim, how do they know that!? Over time we realize that we have helped the process by breaking up the thought forms which then allowed the Light of Heaven through. Getting over the, "I'm the one who did it!" is a process of letting go. It's okay. There is no judgment. In time we realize it is best for all to have this Light; this is what is important. We will always have the next adventure.

We do not need to be in a specific meditative state to transmute darkness. Although, in the beginning this helps center our focus. However, the more adept we become at it, the more we can do it from many places and at many times.

In the beginning stages, we will become aware of the pull in the Collective Consciousness. It will feel heavy, the ideas of the world will haunt us, pull at our attention, cause us to feel angry, or sorrowful. We might find ourselves swept up in a political debate, obsessing about a particular news event. Our attention may be drawn to something that is happening in our neighborhoods, in our schools, in our churches, and even in another country. These emotions are our link. We feel, we pray, we meditate. The way we meditate is not as important as our desire to connect to our I AM Presence, our Spirit. This connection will happen naturally as we call it in, "I AM, I AM. I call the Light of I AM into my mind, body and affairs!" We will be drawn to those things which help us do this. Not everyone will be able to sit quietly for long periods of time, but they may be able to draw or play the piano, even do the dishes. There are as many paths as there are Souls.

Once we are aware of the emotional pull, understand it's makeup, understand the underlying reasons for it's heaviness, the false beliefs, we are ready to dissolve them with Light.

We begin to understand what false beliefs are by questioning them. Is it true that we must know evil in order to know good? Is it true that those who are suffering are suffering because they simply want to experience suffering? What is the Truth of this? It is when we reach into Heaven that we get the Truth. There is always contrast when one is separated from their Spirit. The level of this contrast is dependent upon the consciousness of a Soul and the Collective Consciousness it inhabits. These Souls are not suffering because they want to learn what suffering is. They are suffering because they do not understand how they are manifesting suffering within their lives.

Many feel that if they did not go through a horrible experience, then they would not know what to be grateful for. Really, they are grateful to be out of the horrible experience and do not know how to define that experience with their limited ego mind. Therefore, they use the old Collective Consciousness rationalization of, we need to know the bad in order to appreciate the good. Nonsense.

Angels and other high level Co-creators have volunteered to come here and have experienced very low vibrational incarnations in order to break through these thought forms. Sometimes it seems the more we are capable, the more missions we are sent on. At times I just have to say, I need a vacation!

You will be taught to send, through your intension, Light, to a specific thought form/belief, within the Collective Consciousness. Upon directing Light to it, you will be able dissolve it, or break it apart. The amount of power it takes to do this depends upon the thought form. If you are unskilled in this area or need help, the Archangels are here to assist you. If you feel you do not have the amount of power it takes, you can call for aid from an Archangel and their band of Angels, from a particular teacher in the Heavenly Realms, and/or, the Ascended Host itself.

Your initiation into this arena will come when you have mastered your ego to a high degree. The desire of your Heart will be what gives you power over your ego. Heart energy is the Light energy connected to our Creator.

The first level is deflecting energy. Simply do not give into it. Do not believe in those ideas. Do not believe in those judgments. Simply say, No! This actually creates a powerful boundary the more one is confident in themselves. This is harder for Awakening Angels because it means coming up against the status quo. There is strength in numbers... to a degree. That degree depends upon one's ability to harness Light. The more Awakening Angels connect with who they are, and claim it, the stronger they will become in standing amongst those who are blinded by the shadows in themselves, and the Collective Consciousness at large.

In the second level, one begins to move into larger ideas, judgments, and thought forms. These are the ones that do not like to be told, No. They are stubborn; persistent. We feel them encroaching upon us through our energy grid. They want to attach to us, hang around. We begin to use hand gestures. The people around us may think we are crazy. We flick energy away. We push it away. We clear our auras with our hands by sweeping energy away from ourselves. We may even blow it away by using our breath. We can break up these thought forms through the use of sound. Tones, bells, drums, music, heavenly languages. Even snapping the fingers. You will be able to tell your ability and the strength of your connection by the snapping of fingers. Your determination will come forth through your ability to snap without hesitation. Clapping is another powerful form.

The third level is dissolving a thought form. When one is in a meditative state, one can picture a thought form, this may come as one of those little plays that go on in our head. We see, feel and hear the ideas being projected. For example, if I am aware of something happening in the news, perhaps there is an earthquake, or some type of scandal that is affecting a large number of people, I see this in my mind's eye, and I call forth the Light and ground. Now, one can do this while dancing, this is a very effective method; one I predominantly use. See the situation, and send it Light. Continue to send it light until it is dissolved. You will know it is dissolved because you will feel a completion. The situation will no longer have an intensity to it. In your mind's eye it will have dissipated.

The fourth level is given to those who are able to Wield Light. This is the ability to direct Light like a laser beam. There are many techniques to this and I am not allowed to teach them. I will say this, you will be initiated. You will be taught through Light itself. You will begin to have very high energetic experiences where these types of laser beams will begin to be directed through you. Through various points of Light within you. When you begin to have these experiences, call upon your I AM Presence, the Ascended Host and the Archangels for guidance. You will receive the training because you are ready for it.

*

Angels are not made to reach for grandeur. Although we may be highly fascinated with the growth of our abilities, we do not learn abilities to behave as if we are some egoic idea of a magician or wizard. In many ways, Angels take to the background because we do not like to shine the Light on ourselves. We take our abilities seriously. They are serious. We can do many, many things that can shift the course of consciousness, individually and collectively. It is helpful to know that we will not be given more than we can handle, and if we misuse what we are given, we will lose the ability until we mature. Remember, our desire to Love will always bring us to the right outcome. Even if we fall, the Power of the Light has restorative powers beyond measure. It is our intension, the power of our intension, which is bolstered by the Light of Truth which gives us power.

May our Heavenly Father bless us in the use of this power, to be responsible with it, to trust it, and to desire above all else, to use it in the service of Love. Amen.

There are confirmations given to us when we have transmuted energy. We will experience different types of closure. The dark energy dissipates into nothingness, or there is soft dissolving type of feeling. At other times, a heavier shift takes place. We may also experience, the Showers of Light.

***

SHOWERS OF LIGHT

There comes a point where we are not only highly trained, Wielders of the Light, we are also the, Agents of the Showers of Light.

As Angels on Earth, we have spent much time in the muck and mire, roaming the shadows of the 3rd and 4th Dimensions. We have fought the demons and called for the Light. Held the Light. Defended the Light. Commanded the Light. Because our motive is one of Love, we experience the joy that comes from our service. One way joy is given back to us is through the Showers of Light.

The Showers of Light are very much like fireworks. Everyone ooohs and ahhhs when they see them. Their beauty, the colorful rays of light which expand and explode through the sky cause us to resonate with them in a deeply passionate way. Could it be they are familiar to us? Familiar to the Light within us?

The Showers of Light are seen in the unseen realms. The realms of the 5th Dimension and beyond. They are the result of one's reaching up from the Heart Center through the crown center and into the Heavenly Realms. The Love which is sent from one's being moves straight upward and out of the top of the head. The power of this feeling continues like a beam of light, reaching into the Heavens. It sparks. It ignites. The amount of Love given is the amount of Love sent back in an explosion of Light, beautiful streams of Light pouring down like a fountain cascading over our Souls. They bless the dominion of the one who sent it.

We can intentionally send Showers of Light to groups of people anywhere. When the Light comes back down, we include the consciousness of the area we want it to cover. When I see and feel the beautiful Showers of Light, I think of a particular person, place, or group of Souls. By my attention to them, they receive the Showers of Light with me.

There is also another way the Showers of Light flow down. The Showers of Light come when we have transmuted the sufferings of others within the Collective Consciousness. Our desire to heal the Hearts of men, hail down the Showers of Light. The Light must come when we call it. And when we call it to bless in this way, the Showers of Light manifest with an unspeakable Joy.

What does it mean to take on the suffering of others within the Collective Consciousness? We do this every time we are called to shift those thought forms that are negative in nature. There are levels to this. We can shift our own consciousness by not listening to the ego. We can shift the Collective Consciousness by dissipating thought forms to various degrees.

As explained earlier, we experience the emotions of these thought forms prior to transmuting them, prior to shifting them. Sometimes this is a very painful task. The deeper we tap into the thoughts and feelings of the Collective Consciousness, the deeper we enter that place where the collective pain of Souls are kept. We feel the crying out of Souls across the planet. Depending upon how deep we can go, we may fall on our knees at the sorrow of it. In this we pray and ask for Love to come. There are times when I have pleaded for Love to come. The outpouring of our Hearts to Free the Souls of men is met and the Showers of Light fall into the energetic bodies of those whose Souls were trapped in this darkness, clearing and adding joy.

These Showers of Light, lighten the load. Give a breath of fresh air. Lift vibrations which emanate outward to others. They are tidings of good cheer. We feel it. We remember it. We want it. We seek it.

I hear a voice questioning me. It asks, are you not holding the pattern of suffering by believing it is there? Are you not creating suffering so you can have the experience of saving Souls?

It is not a matter of me believing it is there. I am not asking others to suffer so I can save them. I see it because it is there. I feel it because it is there. I am calling in the Light to break it up. I can call Light because I am able to feel the sorrow which has already been created. It is living in the Astral Plane and has been created on

Earth outside of my beingness; much of it long before I arrived. In my feeling of it and calling in the Light to transmute it, this is what frees up the energy. I do not need to go around creating sorrow in order to heal it. I was sent to Earth in order to heal what is already here.

The above paragraph where I hear a voice questioning me, this is a typical example of the, 'negotiations,' I was talking about earlier. A teaching believed in the Collective Consciousness challenges my authority to override it. When I know who I am and that my mission is sure, aye, I override it.

When one is established in their ability to connect to their crown center, the 7th level of the chakras, many beautiful experiences are had. We begin to reach into the Heavens and experience life there. It is addicting. At times, I have felt a sort of distaste for coming back into the 3rd Dimension. "Yuck, I don't want to be here!" Then I remember I came here so all may experience Heaven's Love.

***

THE HEALING OF OTHERS

There are many Beings who can heal. Co-creators can heal. Masters can heal. Nature Spirits can heal.

Healing requires tuning into specific states of consciousness which reveal the nature of the illness either in the Spiritual, Mental, and/or Emotional Realms. Once the nature of the illness is discovered, to the extent one wants to heal in this area, is to the extent one will be healed. There is no judgment if one chooses not to heal in a specific lifetime. Perhaps they are tired and need a rest before re-embodying and transforming specific beliefs that have held them down. Peace be with them that they know what they are working on and can re-embody with the strength, purpose, and tenacity to shift their consciousness.

There are many healing agents, so to speak, why are Angels known for healing?

Angels, we are specialists in our ability to move through frequencies of Light. This is also what makes us excellent messengers, and why we are known to fly. Because our bodies are finely-tuned to the various dimensions, we can quickly see where blockages occur, something that Co-creators learn, often times through Angels.

Since Angels can move through dimensions, we have access to higher frequencies of Light that we can step down, and direct.

Nature spirits sooth, and through their healing rays, can help one listen to their own Heart, mind and emotions, so that they can shift states of consciousness on their own. There are many messengers in the Nature Spirits, and in all of the Elements, that will assist in our raising of consciousness, which is what healing is; if we are willing to listen. We can receive energy from nature by touching a tree, walking barefoot through the grass, putting our feet in a pond, or gazing up at the stars. Nature restores us simply because it gives energy. The more one creates a relationship to Nature, the more one becomes aware of its peaceful and graceful energy. Nature Spirits remember us, and look forward to our communicating with them. It is also important to note that Nature Spirits have been here a very long time. They have many lessons to teach us if we are open.

Masters are often very busy helping Co-creators get a handle on who they are and what they are doing, as you can see from the current state of our planet, this keeps the Masters very busy indeed, and though they are able to heal, they often assign the many Angels who are created for this purpose.

We are called to heal Souls who do not know how to heal on their own. We are called to comfort and guide. Some of us have decided to join the healing professions, whether in traditional ways, or in more esoteric ways.

Some of us heal on an as needed basis. We may be sent to the store and be directed to a person there. We may be sitting in the theatre and feel the energy of a person asking for help there. For those of us who heal in this way, our techniques will be different, for obvious reasons. At times we may touch someone and give them Light, and there may be times when we simply send it to them, adjusting the grids as needed.

Let me take a moment to discuss the aspect of touch. When we touch we transfer energy. There will be times when we do not want to transfer energy. This is acceptable. We may not have the energy to give at that particular moment. We may be percolating. If we do touch someone, perhaps we are saying hello to a neighbor and we touch their hand, we will know right away if we have suffered some form of energy loss. The immediate remedy is to wipe the area of contact and seal the leakage. We can easily do this with our hand and then wipe our hands onto our clothing or nearby object such as a wall, or fence. If we pick up someone's energy during this time, we must whisk it away by shaking our hands into the air. A simple flip of the hands is generally all that is needed. You will know when you have accomplished the task because your energy will be restored. We must clear ourselves as quickly as possible because we are in the process of filling our well and cannot spend time in energetic exchanges that interfere with this process. Protecting our energy is not only vital for our health, it is vital for our mission.

Angels who are in the healing professions on a more full-time basis have a high ability of maintaining balance. They are able to maintain their level of Light in the more denser realms of manifestation. They are capable of shifting the energy of one person, then an hour later, shift another person's energy. They can do this frequently throughout the day without getting caught in any one person's energetic field. Bless them. They work hard on keeping their own energy clear by keeping themselves grounded, clearing their own field of any picked up energies, and by taking time off when need be. One simply cannot give what they do not have to give. It is imperative for healers to rest, and recharge.

Being natural healers, Angels who move into these professions learn quickly the various modalities that are taught in order to facilitate healing. If one finds themselves in the energetic fields of healing, they will be surprised at how fast they pick it up and create their own ways of moving through the energetic grids.

There is not only one way to move through the grids. Some healers are visual, and some are sensate. Some are able to shift energy through tone and sound.

*

When one begins to learn about the energetic grids, they can be lead to teachers who can teach techniques. These are valuable to learn. It is important to study the energy systems well in order to fully understand how they function. While learning these systems, be open to new information. Connecting to your I AM Presence, other Angels, and the Ascended Host, will help you tremendously. They will show you things you will not read in books. They will give you experiences of your own. You will discover the best way to move into an energetic field by using your innate abilities, be they visual, sensate or auditory. You will create your own techniques. The creation of these techniques comes through being sensitive to energy itself and how skilled one is in moving, or harnessing it. By practicing, and seeing the results, your confidence will grow.

When I was in energy healing school, I would call upon the Angels to assist me. At times I saw them, at others I didn't. However, I could always feel what they were doing as they were using my body as a vehicle to deliver the energy here or there. They did not need me to do this. They used my vehicle in order to show me how to take in energy and work with it.

There comes a point when we do not need to touch a person in order to shift their energy. The power of our mind will have become so strong that we can merely think it and it is done. This may sound pompous, but it is true. Intension does not require a specific channel in order to deliver the results. Energy is energy. The shifting of it comes from our focus upon it, and our intension to shift it. The power of our consciousness, the power of our Light is all that is needed. This type of healing occurs when the person is ready for it. If they want it but are not ready for an instant manifestation of it, which is often the case, we can shift it now, and they may be ready for the fullness of it a year from now. We can shift the energy by surrounding it in a cocoon of Light for safe keeping. The cocoon will slowly release energy while the Soul is moving into a new level of awareness and can safely, over time, welcome the changes that this awareness brings.

Shifting energy anywhere in a Souls energy field will cause a shift in their perception. As we circulate energy through their energy bodies, the stuck energy begins to move and dissipate. Higher frequencies of Light take its place and a balanced, freer flow of energy is felt throughout the body as it adjusts to its new level of vibration and consciousness.

As this new Light moves through them it raises their consciousness. We must respect their process by not pushing our Light onto or into them. With Love as our guide, we will be sensitive to these issues and know how to handle them as they arise. Discussing how they feel after the healing will help us guide them further to ensure they are able to continue to hold this new level of Light, this new level of consciousness.

We may have several Souls that we are working with on the inner planes. We can touch in and out of their fields as they call us. We know they are calling us when we feel their energy, or see an image of them in our mind's eye. In that moment, we can send them Light. If there is a larger request, we can attend to them when we are able to focus more directly on their field.

It is important to not allow others to continually contact us in order to take energy from us. We will know when this is happening and we must protect our energy borders. We learn that we give as we are lead to give, not out of pity, not out of obligation. It is imperative we learn this because we can spend a lot of time in endeavors we are not meant to be caught up in. Allowing others to siphon off our energy aides them in avoiding responsibility for their own life, and prohibits their growth. It can also drain us and cause depression, and anxiety. Our own levels will be weakened, and we will be more susceptible to the pull of the negative energies within the Collective Consciousness.

We may get sucked in from time to time helping these areas, however, we must realize in doing so we may be ignoring the mission we are meant to be on. This is more difficult for an Awakening Angel who is learning to discern between their desire to serve and their call to serve.

There will be times when another comes to you for healing, and you find they do not truly want healing. They are afraid of the shift in consciousness that will come. Their holding onto their current state of consciousness is what has caused their modality, yet, they are not yet ready to face the Truth of their situation. In this regard, there is nothing you can do but bless them and send them on their way.

Sometimes we will want to distance heal another, such as a loved one. When we touch into their field, we may sense a block. If we cannot connect into their field, we must respectfully withdraw. This may feel painful at times, particularly when we know another suffers. We can ask other Angels to protect and heal them. The Angels we send in these endeavors are not Angels living on Earth but Angels living in the higher dimensions. They are able to move into and through the 4th and 5th Dimensions easily and they are happy to serve in this way. By doing this we can feel confident that our loved ones are taken care of and we can let go.

It is important for us to let go. Not only for ourselves, but for others. If we are constantly knocking on the door of their energy field, they can feel overwhelmed and become resistant. The opposite of what is wanted. If we are not the Angel for the job, we are not the Angel for the job and that is all there is to it. Trust. Soon, one realizes they are not meant to do everything. Once we trust and are willing to let go, it is like a big exhale that takes the weight off and we can go make some popcorn and watch a good movie knowing full well we will be lead to our next assignment.

***

RESPONSIBLE MANIFESTING

Generally, on Planet Earth, we've been taught to focus on particular things. How to manifest the career we want. The car we want. The house. We manifest them and we are happy for a time and then we feel we are lacking. Something is missing. The lyrics, "Money can't buy you love," begin to ring in our heads.

Things do not fill the void. They do not fill the void because in and of themselves, they are not what we are looking for.

Some say we are here to manifest bigger and better things. That we came into this world with the express reason to experience life in the 3rd Dimension.

Currently, the Souls on Earth did not come here to merely experience manifesting in the 3rd Dimension. They have been so out of touch with their ability to manifest, they do not even know why they are here. They have no real idea how they got here, nor any real idea of how to get back home. They are here because their level of consciousness brought them here. So it is from here they must raise their level of consciousness.

The whole point of creation is growth. Creation *is* growth. If you are not creating you are retracting. Our creations are sustainable when they are made from the consciousness of Truth. The consciousness of Truth is predominantly formless; comprised of virtues. While it is true one can experiment with being separated from one's I AM Presence, and our Creator, one was never meant to dissociate to such a degree where one almost completely loses track of who they are. Sinking down to this level of manifestation has no benefit. We do not need to suffer to this degree, where it becomes morbid and crosses others Free Will. If you want a picture of hell, a form of hell, turn on the news; murder, rape, slaughter, war, famine, these are aspects of hell. Do we need to see the flames?

False gods and idols are egoic forms. We are not to build these forms which take us away from our Creator, nor ourselves, to the degree where we lose ourselves almost completely. To tell one they are here simply to experience being here is to keep them in a locked state of mind with no way out. When one has manifested a number of experiences, one begins to wonder, what else is there? They are certainly not looking for more of the same, which is what happens in the 3rd Dimension, because it is the 3rd Dimension. This is why they say, bring Heaven to Earth.

We will never not manifest, so there is no question we will always be creating more. More of what is the question.

If one merely manifests from egoic ideas of life, they will receive these manifestations. They tend to be of a low level of vibration and this is why we feel empty after a certain point. The Light of who we are, no matter how dim it may be, is always desiring to expand. It cannot expand by using 3rd Dimensional ideas. It expands by desiring Higher Ideals. Ideals from the 5th Dimension and up.

The ego can only manifest what it knows. It knows a very limited playing field. Go to the grocery store and look at the magazines there. This is the playing field the ego knows. The world of what you see is what you get. We are trained to get more and more of the finer things, those things which we get approved of by others who manifest through the use of ego. It becomes a race to the top of ego gratification. Those who are not in the race, or feel intimidated by the race, are judged because they have not achieved the same level of ego gratification as others.

As Angels, it is our responsibility to break away from the conditioned mind-set of limiting manifestations on the 3rd Dimension. We must recognize that we are here on a mission. Our mission is not to bask in the rays of Earthly creations, our mission is to add Light to the planet so the Souls in this realm can reach up to the 5th Dimension and free themselves from the egoic thinking which separated them from their I AM Presence, and our Creator.

***

CHAPTER III
ANGELIC PRAYERS

*In all they do, Angels are drawn to the Light.
Drawn to bring the Light out in others,
and drawn to bring the Light down to Earth.*

CALLING AND CLAIMING ONE'S ANGELIC I AM PRESENCE

In the name of I AM, I AM. I call forth the Light and Truth of Love and all that is Holy. I call forth and Claim my Angelic I AM Presence. I hold to my Presence as the True Source of my Life. I am willing to leave behind all egoic lies and desires in order to embrace the Truth of who I AM in the Light.

I AM (Angelic name) I AM.
I AM (Angelic name) I AM.
I AM (Angelic name) I AM.

I am an Angel. A High Being of Light created to serve my Creator and the Heavenly Realms. Created to serve the One and the Many.

I Claim my Angelic Heritage and I Bless all Life.

I Call Forth the Light to fill me and I Accept this Light as the Truth of my Life.

I Call Forth Protection from the Heavenly Realms, and the Angelic Kingdoms.

I Call Forth the White Light of Truth to clear my Aura and my energetic bodies.

I Call forth Wisdom and Guidance that I may serve through the portal of my Heart and be a Blessing to all that is True.

As Above, so Below.

Blessed be our Creator, our Love; the Most High.
Blessed be the Angels who serve our Love and Light.
Amen and Amen.

THE ENTRANCEWAY OF THE HEART

Blessed My Holy Mother and Father, Creator of all that is, how beautiful you are. Oh Holy Love, please help me feel love inside my heart, to know you as my one true creator, to see past the veils of dimensions, to touch my heart that it may be open for as much as I can handle right now. Please help me to always remember to listen to my heart. Amen and Amen.

DISCERNMENT AND WISDOM

Father-Mother God, I bring myself before you, asking for a Blessing of your Divine Wisdom. Open my eyes to see Truth. Guide me to the Open Fields.
Pour your Light upon me that I may see and not be afraid. Pour your Light upon me and let Wisdom Shine through my body. Pour your Light upon me; let Wisdom Reign.

Bless you and thank you, oh Loving Lord.
Amen and Amen.

DESIRE TO FORGIVE

Sweet Holy Father, I pray, help me to want to forgive this (person/situation) and see the higher reasons of why my consciousness brought this into my life. Help me to learn my part, whether fear, judgment or other that I may forgive myself for drawing this to me and to release the other that I may be free.

DISSOLVING FEAR

Holy Father Whom Art All Creation, thank you for creating me as a part of yourself. Help me to realize you are my Shepard and I shall not want. You go before me, to make my way clear. Open my eyes, dear Lord, that I may see your magnificence in everyday of my life, that I may understand duality and whom you are in it. With this I know, what do I have to fear when you created me and all of creation. Thank you, Amen and Amen.

RELEASING EXPECTATIONS & ACCEPTANCE

My Holy Father Whom Art All Creation, I pray, dear Lord, that my eyes be opened; that my heart be opened to see my ego expectations and accept they are merely my perception of the world; what I want based upon my own reasoning. I know we were given each our own desire to be whom you created us to be. Help me accept myself as you created me. Help me be bold and strong to live as you created me. Help me to love others as you created even their souls. Oh, Holy Father, help me to understand the way I have been programmed to see the world is not how you see the world; and you can make anything happen at any time. Help me let go and embrace your love for me. Help me let go and see you have the whole light of the universe, what is a miracle to us is natural to you. Bless you, Holy Father, thank you for knowing what is best for me, blessing me with what is best for me, but mostly, by blessing me to know the difference between ego expectations and Spirit's higher wisdom. Amen and Amen.

REMOVING DARK ENERGIES

I pray, in the name of All that is Pure and Holy to bring light to this _____. Keep me ever watchful, knowing any dark energies are coming from lower vibrations, and in our Creator's Kingdom they do not exist. They cannot exist in the Light of All of Creation. There is no match for our Holy Creator as these energies are not of him, and when I stand in the Light of Love, they cannot touch me. You are my Shepard Pure and Holy Love, and thus I know, my faith is renewed in your light.

PROTECTION

Holy Angels, protect (me/person/situation) coming and going, protect others and bless (person/situation) Please move me as is best for me to be moved, speak through me as needed to bless and keep myself aware of our Creator's being. Bring me the Light and Revelation of our Lord, as I can handle, and bless you for all you have done for me.

MARY'S HEART FOR A PEACEFUL HOME

I call upon the Pink Heart Light of Mary.

I ask that you Enter and Bless our home with your Gentle Kiss of Love.

Radiate your Light and sooth the edges; bring healing to the Secret Places.

May our Hearts be Open to receive your Love and Strength.

I Bless you for your Presence Mary, accept this gift of my Love.
(take a moment to express your inner gratitude)

I seal this prayer in the Golden White Light of the Heavens.

Amen & Amen.

CHAPTER IV

THE LITTLE GLASS MERMAID
A Story

I saw a little glass mermaid. It was so tiny and sweet, yellow and it had such a beautiful and delicate dazzling fin.

When I got home I put it on the table next to my goldfish bowl.

Oh, I did not know how much she wanted to be in that bowl.

To swim with her friends like her family did in the sea.

She would try to send out telepathic signals to me, but I was distracted, scurrying about my business.

She would try to move her little glass body, always falling over when I fixed the table linen.

Then one day, a little girl came over with her brother. They were staring at my goldfish, Fred. Then the little girl whispered to the little boy, "Let's put the mermaid inside the tank." He looked at her with his eyes wide with excitement. He lunged at the little mermaid but his sister got to her first. "It was my idea."

"Shhh." said the brother

I could hear them but I did not think anything bad would happen and so I let them do it.

The little girl, Sarah, carefully and most gently placed the little mermaid on top of the water, and let go of her.

The little glass mermaid began to sink, not realizing she was now where she had wanted to be.

Immediately, she began to swim. It took her awhile to break free from the glass, and she was worried her gils would not open up in time. But she made it. As soon as she decided she was not going to give up this opportunity, the glass slipped away from her and melted in the water.

And there was Fred, looking in all amazement. "You made it, little glass mermaid, I knew you would, as soon as you made up your mind."

For the little glass mermaid it was like the sea. Her tiny and sweet body fit perfectly. And when I knew how much she loved to be there, and how her fins sparkled with light. I made a home for her out of rocks, and planted some underwater flowers and trees.

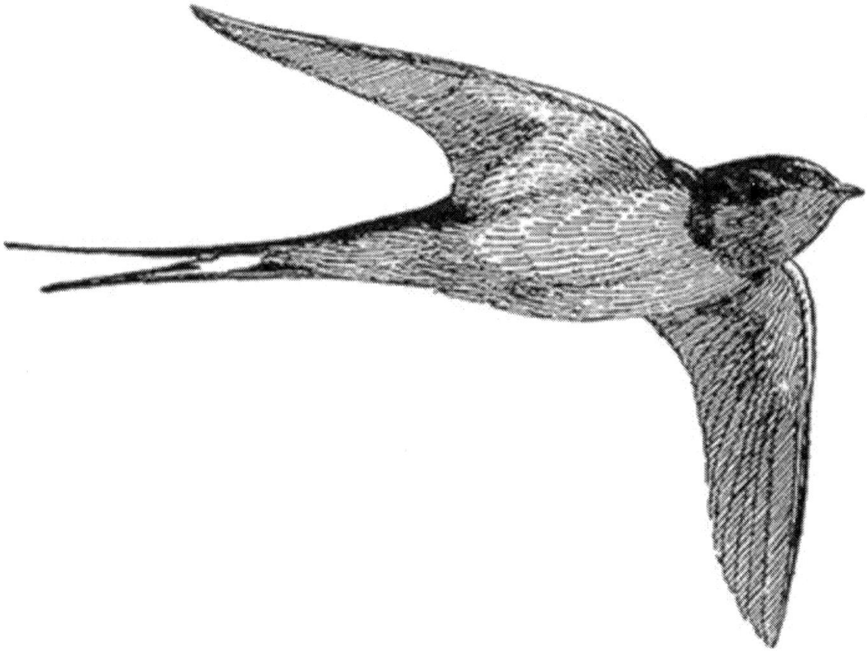

Made in the USA
Columbia, SC
19 December 2024